# Gracie.......

## IRON RANGE COOKING WITH AN ITALIAN MOTHER

## PASTA TO POTICA

A Compilation of recipes used by a renowned cook, who owned a catering service and restaurant in Virginia, Minnesota for 35 years.

Published by:
Patreas Publications
Northland Printing
501 2nd Avenue
Two Harbors, Minnesota 55616-1509

Third Printing December 1997

*About the author:*

Sharon Ceryance DeLeo is the eldest child of Grace Gingerelli Ceryance.

Sharon shares her mother's love of cooking and also loves antiques. She and her husband, David, have a restaurant/antique shop called Shari's Kitchen & Carousel Antiques located in Two Harbors, MN, on the shores of beautiful Lake Superior.

She wrote this book to share with family members and friends, the recipes that her mother used to create the memorable ethnic cuisine of the Iron Range of Northeast Minnesota. This book is made of ethnic culinary delights that should not be lost to future generations.

Dear Hedy,

Hope you enjoy my family recipes and stories.

Mille Grazie!

Sharon

# GRACIE.......

## IRON RANGE COOKING WITH AN ITALIAN MOTHER

## PASTA TO POTICA

## INTRODUCTION

This is not just a "cookbook", it is a tribute to a woman whose entire life was motivated by food. My mother lived to cook. Grace Gingerelli Ceryance's name was synonymous with good tasting food. One of ten children, her mother became paralyzed after a cerebral hemorrhage when Gracie was only fourteen years old. Gracie and her sister, Florence (nicknamed Peenie) had to assume the responsibility of cooking for the family. It was the middle of the "Great Depression". There were numerous gardens to tend, pigs to feed, preserves to put up for winter. Three hard working brothers and an aged, lonely father were always hungry. Every few days 25 pounds of flour had to be made into bread. There was no such thing as "store bought" bread or bakery. Mother once told me that she dreamed of eating bakery bread, but they dared not spend the money on such a frivolous item. After two years of struggling to cope with attending school and trying to help run a household, she decided to drop out of school. She always told me that she was heartbroken when she had to quit going to school, but with a demanding, immigrant father life was very difficult. They didn't communicate well. He wanted his children to speak English, therefore, didn't encourage them to speak Italian. The three older children could speak Italian, but they already had moved away from home; busy with their own families.

This book is not about ordinary food. It is composed of old fashioned recipes and ethnic recipes that, at first glance, may seem too complicated to handle. If this scares you, this is not the book for you. But if you're interested in the culture and heritage of the Iron Range and what makes up some of it's people, this is the book for you. The cooking of ethnic foods is becoming a lost art. Stretching a potica completely over a kitchen table is something special to watch or do. Mother didn't want to see this art die. She so badly wanted to share her knowledge of good cooking with the world. In a way, she missed her calling, she should have been a chef training people in the culinary arts, but she was just happy cooking for all of her customers who came into her restaurant and loved her "Dago Soup", or her fabulous rigatonis and meatballs. Every time she tried a new soup recipe and loved it, she would squeal with delight just like a kid who discovered a favorite candy. Her customers loved her. If someone couldn't afford to pay to eat, of course, she fed them anyway. She was probably most proud of her walnut poticas. During the holidays, just before Thanksgiving, a list would start at the restaurant. They would lose count of how many poticas had to be made. They would ship poticas all over the country. She kept track of the poticas according to how many cases of walnuts had to be ordered. One of her customers labeled her, "The Potica Queen of the Iron Range". She would truly grieve if you didn't receive one of her poticas for your holiday celebration. She always wanted to make everyone happy, and in her mind, food was the key to happiness. She never attended a family dinner or celebration without bringing along some kind of food, whether or not you asked for it. I tried to write this book in my mother's words, but she was such a natural cook that it was difficult to get exact recipes from her. When you cooked with Gracie, only she knew how many people a recipe would feed. There was never a lack of food in her home, in fact she always cooked too much. Cooks like Gracie just knew how a dough felt, or what it might need to make it taste better, or how to stretch a dish to feed drop-in company. These are skills that can never go into a cook book, or be written down on paper; this type of cooking is truly an art. Like Michelangelo or Rembrandt where painting was innate, that's how Gracie was with food.

Being a liberated woman is such an issue today. And, during the years, I've read very negative articles on how the women on the Iron Range were treated by the men. I know where I was raised, it wasn't in that kind of household. Mother was a true matriarch of the family. We always thought it was because of her Italian heritage. My father was of Croatian descent and very easy going. There was never an issue of "who" was going to run things. In fact, all of mother's friends were the kinds of ladies who "ran the house-holds", so I am often surprised when I read these articles. Most evenings, our house was filled with her lady friends talking and comparing notes as to who had the whitest wash, how long it took them to do their chores for that day, swap-ping recipes, the amount of ironing they had to tackle before they could start dinner, and simply sharing whatever it was that turned their cranks or bothered their souls. This was long before support groups. Neighborhood women were their own support groups. As a very young child, my observation of mother and her friends was that these women took pride in their housekeeping . They felt that it was very rewarding to have made a fabulous meatloaf for supper, or a simply luscious dessert, heaped with real whipped cream. Their self esteem was totally dependent upon their homemaking skills. I know that as a society, things have really changed, but women were happy pleasing their families. Cooking starts with planning, writing a good shopping list, and set-ting aside a certain amount of time. With a few organiza-tional skills, by planning ahead and freezing, one can serve a fabulous "company dinner" without feeling over-whelmed. Advance preparation keeps the mess out of the kitchen on "the day" and you will feel very organized and effi-cient. Advance preparation will also allow you to arrange a beautiful table; using the dishes you received as a wedding present just sitting on a shelf getting dusty, or using your grandmother's best china that you inherited and have never used because you are in such a rush you're afraid of breaking them. Entertaining doesn't have to be a hassle or expensive. If you don't have pretty dishes or candle holders, check out antique shops or discount stores where some pretty bargain pieces may be hiding. Candles and a few cut flowers are inexpensive. Remember, when entertaining, presentation is everything. Food should taste as good as it looks, a nice garnish helps that along, a delicious dessert can top off any meal, and certainly good coffee is a must. With all the flavored coffees available that should be no problem. But always serve coffee in a china cup, it enhances any coffee. A beautifully set table helps provide the ambiance, and now you're all set to "wow" your friends with your skills.

I feel lucky to have been raised by a mother who loved food and cooking. I am the oldest of five children who were all made to feel special. Our birthdays were celebrations that royalty would covet. My hope is that this cookbook will make you feel you not only learned something about food, but enjoyed reading about the accomplishments of a woman who manifested her love of family and friends through the joy of cooking.

Bon Appetite

Sharon Ceryance DeLeo

GRACIE'S FIRST HOLY COMMUNION AGE 7.

**THE HAPPY NEWLYWEDS IN 1939.
GRACIE & FUTZ**

# TABLE OF CONTENTS

# HELPFUL HINTS

◊ To prevent food smears on recipes, make a copy or cover with plastic while cooking.

◊ When boiling pasta, always put oil and salt in the water to prevent noodles from sticking; plus salt make the water come to a boil faster. Be sure to cover with a lid until boiling , then remove the lid.

◊ Melt butter, margarine, cheese, chocolate, or any food that is to be melted , in the microwave; it saves a mess with a pan on top of the stove, and eliminates the scraping of a pan that is very difficult to clean.

◊ When adding milk to thin out cream soups, always heat the milk first. Adding cold milk to a hot soup will immediately spoil it.

◊ The same tip includes water. Always heat your water before adding it to a hot broth or hot meat. Adding cold water to a hot meat will make the meat tough.

◊ It is not necessary to salt beef. Beef has it's own natural salt, and adding salt tends to make beef tough.

◊ To ensure freshness of nuts, store in tightly covered container in refrigerator.

◊ To save a left over onion, put a little butter on the half before refrigerating; it will stay fresh longer.

◊ To prevent fruit pie crust from becoming soggy, brush the bottom with a bit of egg white before adding filling.

◊ When cooking beans in broth, be sure the beans are fully cooked before adding any other ingredient as they take so long to cook.

◊ To thicken blueberries for pie filling, add 2 table-spoons of tapioca.

◊ Bisquick is quicker and makes a "never fail" bis-cuit. If you run out of Bisquick, you can make your own: Mix together 8 cups of flour ,1/4 cup of bak-ing powder, 1 teaspoon salt, and 1 cup of shorten-ing. Store in airtight container. When needed, mix with a little milk for your biscuits.

◊ When cooking sauerkraut, add a little bit of grated potatoes; it gives it more bulk.

◊ After baking is out of oven, remove from pans onto cooling racks, or set entire pan on cooling rack, such as pies, etc. Cooling racks are neces-sary components to proper food handling. Improp-erly cooled foods will change the texture and, ulti-mately, the taste

◊ Proper freezing procedures are very important. Do not freeze together items that should be used individually, for instance: hamburger patties, cookies, pasta, cheese, pork chops, or any items that you would want to use quickly.

Method: Lay individual items on a cookie sheet. Freeze solidly. Remove from sheet then stack in covered container with waxed paper between. Pasta, such as raviolis or gnocchi, can be frozen raw then placed into boiling water while it is still frozen. Cooked pasta, such as spaghetti, can be frozen in a lump then placed into boiling water while still frozen. Don't ever throw away left over pastas or rice; always freeze until ready for next use.

◊ Removal of starch from pasta: boil pasta to al-denté, which is a little firm, slowly run cold water into the pot until the pasta is cold and all starch is removed. Drain, set aside until ready to use. When ready to use, heat another pot of water to boiling, insert a strainer to properly fit inside; submerge cold spaghetti into fresh boiling water for about 2-3 minutes, remove in strainer, shake excess water by banging strainer onto a towel, immediately add to your hot sauce.

◊ When a recipe calls for kneading or cutting in shortening, use a dough hook. It's worth buying a mixer that has a hook attachment to save labor and for a nicer texture.

◊ A food processor is another valuable kitchen aide for chopping and grinding.

◊ To ensure the best baking results, pre-heat your oven and have your rack on center level.

◊ To ensure the best baking textures, do not change the fats; if a recipe calls for butter, or margarine, or shortening, or oil, use it. Substitution will change the texture. Some people believe that only butter is better, but that's not necessarily true when it comes to texture. The taste of butter may be better, but it may be too rich for certain items.

# Anise Biscuits- Biscotti

Serving Size : 48

| | |
|---|---|
| 6 | eggs |
| 1 1/2 | cups sugar |
| 1 | cup milk |
| 1 | teaspoon anise seed |
| 1 | teaspoon vanilla |
| 1 | teaspoon salt |
| 8 | cups flour |
| 5 | teaspoons baking powder |
| 1/2 | pound butter |

Cream together sugar & butter. Add remaining ingredients to form a stiff dough. Roll out dough to 1/4" thickness. Cut with a small round biscuit cutter. ( While baking, they should rise & double in size.) Bake on lightly greased baking sheet at 375 º for 10 minutes. Remove immediately and cool on cooling racks. After completely cooled, frost with powdered sugar frosting (see recipe). Frost them very thickly, and if desired, tint with colors.

- - - - - - - - - - - - - - - - -

NOTES : This is a fabulous cookie. It is Italian for biscuit, hence the cutting with a biscuit cutter. We call them, "biscotti". Today most people think of biscotti as the hard, almond topped cookies. These are very Italian and as far as I know, have been around a lot longer than the others. For celebrations, we would frost them with a heavy powdered sugar frosting and tint the frosting different colors, such as red & green for Christmas, or pastels for Easter or weddings. None of our family celebrations were ever served without our biscotti as one of the desserts.

# Antipasto

Serving Size : 12

| | |
|---|---|
| 1 | head cauliflower — flowered |
| 2 | pounds carrots — sliced 1/4" thick |
| 2 | cans Italian beans |
| 2 | cans tuna fish |
| 1 | can black olives |
| 1 | can  green olives |
| 2 | cups  spaghetti sauce |

Place two quarts water in large kettle, par boil carrots. Add cauliflower to carrots, continue boiling until both are cooked. (carrots take longer to cook, cauliflower is cooked in a few minutes)  If too much water is left, drain some.  Leave about a cup of water to help mix in the sauce.  Add all other ingredients.  So as not to break up the cauliflower, mix together gently with a large rubber scraper.

- - - - - - - - - - - - - - - - - -

Serving Ideas : Appetizer with your favorite Italian meal.

NOTES : Antipasto can be bottled and stored on a shelf.  My Auntie Peenie had only one child, therefore, she bottled hers.  With our large family of eight, at dinner time, mother just put the bowlful on the table and it was gone in one sitting.  All of the kids in our family are fast eaters; we sort of gobble up our food.  I always tell people, "When you are growing up and eating at a table with eight people, you must eat quickly in order to get enough."  There was rarely a left-over for our old cocker spaniel, "Skipper", who sat faithfully under the table eagerly awaiting a bit of food to fall from our plates.

# Apple Potica

Serving Size : 30

|       |                                   |
|-------|-----------------------------------|
| 3     | cups  flour — level               |
| 1     | teaspoon salt                     |
| 1     | egg                               |
| 1     | tablespoon oil                    |
| 1     | cup water — warm                  |
| 3     | pounds apples — peeled and sliced |
| 1 1/2 | cups sugar                        |
| 3     | tablespoons cinnamon              |
| 1/4   | pound butter — melted             |

Make a well in dry ingredients, add liquids, mix all together (best if mixed with a dough hook). Keep working dough till it forms a ball. Turn onto floured cloth & knead dough till it shapes into a nice, pliable ball (it takes about 5 minutes). Place dough in well oiled bowl and cover tightly. Let dough rest for 4 hours. When dough is ready, lay a clean tablecloth or sheet on a rectangular table.  Sprinkle flour over entire cloth.  Place dough in center of table and start pulling from the underside, pulling gently so as not to tear holes in the dough. Stretch dough over entire table & let a couple of inches hang down on all sides to help anchor the dough. Dough will be transparent.  (You must work quickly so the dough doesn't dry out and become flaky). Lay apples over 2/3 of the area. Sprinkle with sugar and cinnamon. Pour on melted butter.  Trim 3 edges to edge of table, leaving one lengthwise edge long, but trim heavy ridge off all 4 sides of dough with a sharp knife.  Flap the one long edge of "over hanging" dough over the apples; this allows a start for your potica roll. Lift the cloth under this start area and as you lift the cloth, the dough will start rolling itself. Lift the cloth slowly and keep pulling the cloth toward you so the potica doesn't fall off the table. Fold excess dough, which is now on the ends, under the whole strip. Lay the potica strip onto a well-greased jelly roll pan in a "paper clip" fashion. Bake in preheated 350 º oven for 1 to 1 1/2 hours or until golden brown. As the potica is baking, you may baste it with it's own juice. Cool before removing from the pan, however, keep an eye on it, if there is too much loose syrup in the pan, the potica will stick and be difficult to remove. Potica may be assembled and put into the freezer unbaked for future use. To do this, cover unbaked potica with a buttered waxed paper to prevent sticking to soft dough, then cover completely with aluminum foil, then label. Freeze until needed. Not necessary to thaw before baking. Just uncover and bake as directed. A variety of poticas may be made with this dough, cheese potica (a recipe will be on another page), blueberry, lemon, or even tuna fish.

- - - - - - - - - - - - - - - - - - - - - -

Notes: When we were growing up, being Catholic meant having to abstain on Fridays, so mother often made us a tuna fish potica for dinner and then apple potica for dessert. Cottage cheese potica was also made as a meal. Apple potica was a must at all of our holidays, weddings, or any special celebration. From the eldest relative to the youngest, I can honestly say that "Apple Potica" is a favorite dish of this family. Even the little grandchildren clap their hands with joy when they see apple potica.

STEP 1:    The potica dough in a bowl ready
           to rest.

STEP 2:    Stretching the dough over a table
           by pulling from the underside.  It
                   must be paper thin and
           transparent.

STEP 3:    Laying the apples, sugar, and
           cinnamon over the stretched out
                   dough.

STEP 4:    Pouring butter over the entire
           potica.

STEP 5:    Rolling the dough by lifting the
           tablecloth.

STEP 6:    The successful roll....it stayed on
           the table and did not roll onto the
           floor.

STEP 7:    Finally the apple potica is coiled
           in the pan, ready for baking.
           Gracie is one of four generations
           who helped make this potica.
           Daughters, granddaughters,
           great-grand daughters, a niece,
           a sister-in-law,  and a daughter-
           in-law are pictured  with her.

STEP: 1

STEP: 2

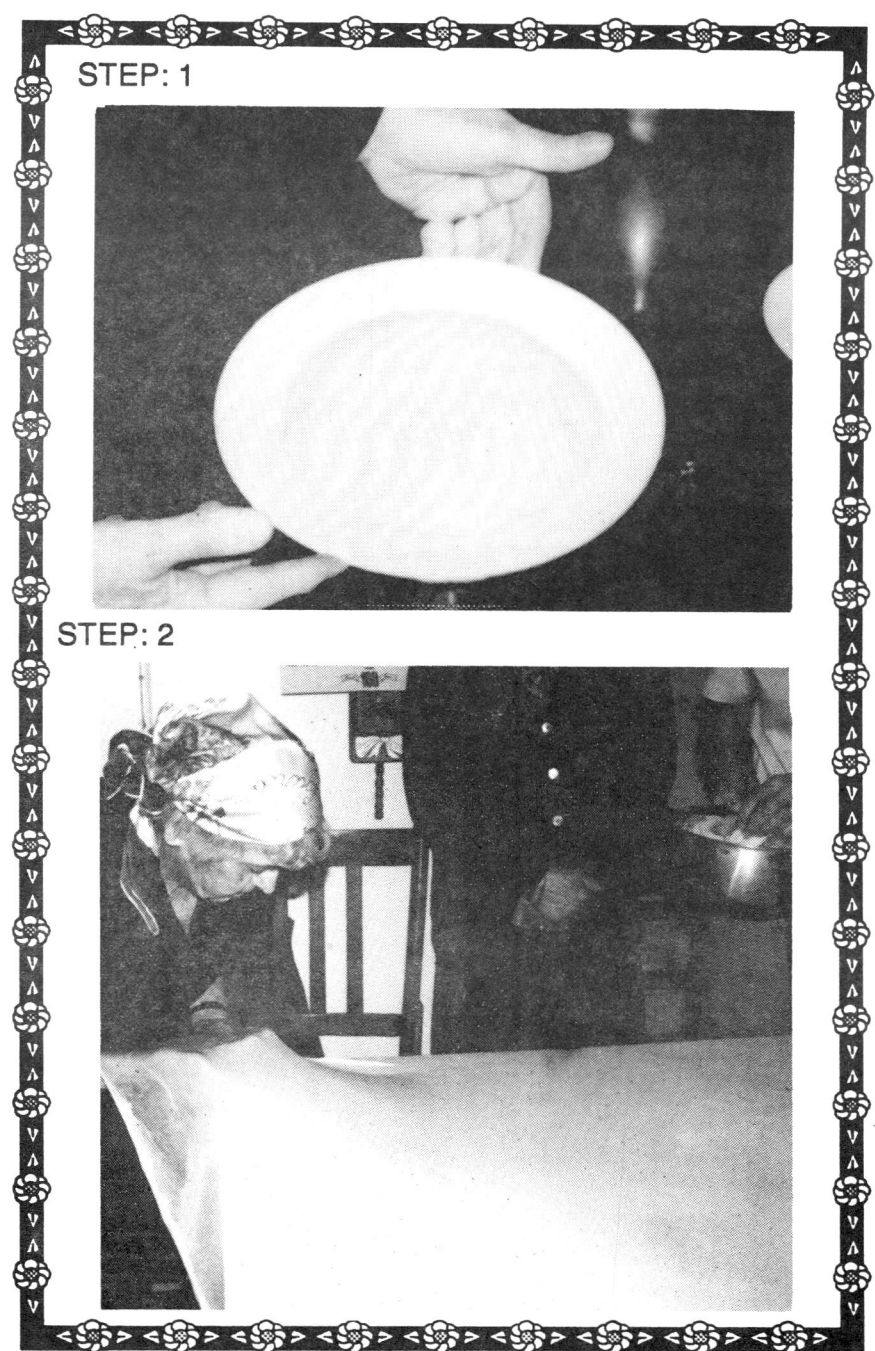

STEP: 3

STEP: 4

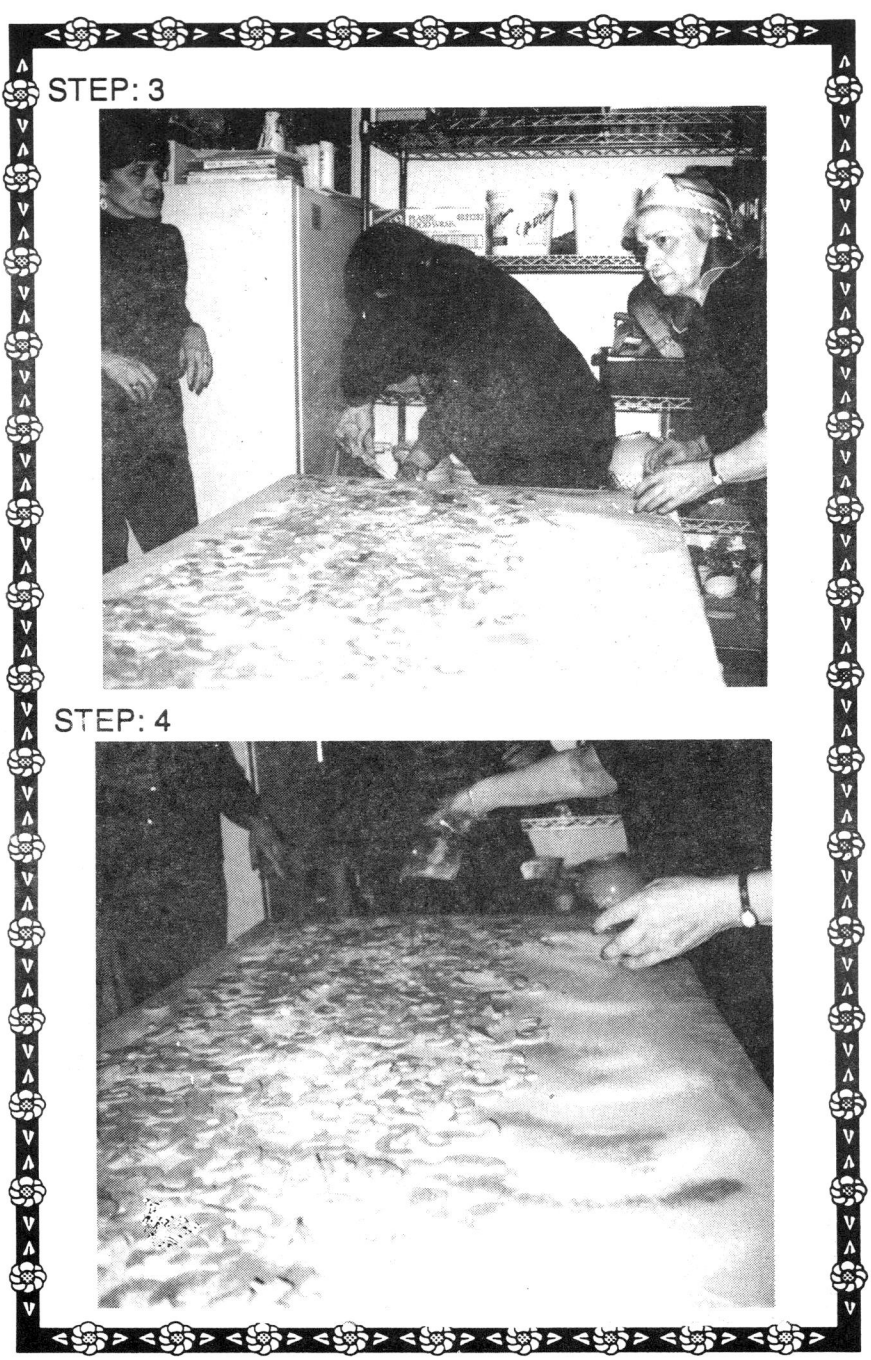

**STEP: 5**

**STEP 6**

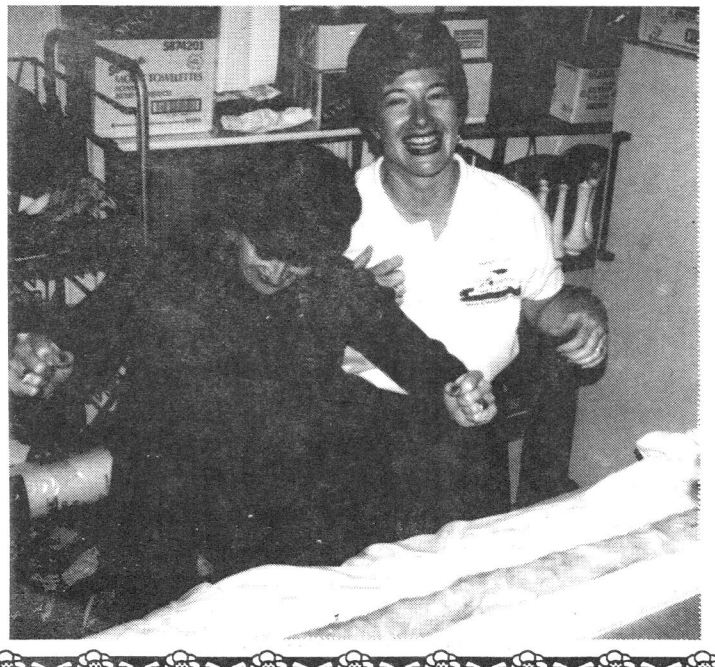

23

STEP: 7

Back Row: Sister-in-law Irene Gingerelli and granddaughter Jackie Phifer. Second Row: Daughter Sharon DeLeo, great-granddaughter Leah Phifer, daughter Barbara Groves, niece Carolyn Gingerelli, granddaughter Sarah Lundgren, and daughter-in-law Shelly Ceryance. Front Row: Great-granddaughter Kasey Phifer and Gracie.

# Canelake's Chunk o' Chocolate Cookie

Serving Size : 36

|       |                                          |
|-------|------------------------------------------|
| 1     | cup shortening                           |
| 3/4   | cup brown sugar — packed                 |
| 3/4   | cup sugar                                |
| 3     | eggs                                     |
| 4     | cups flour                               |
| 1     | teaspoon baking powder                   |
| 3     | tablespoons water — boiling              |
| 1 1/4 | teaspoons soda                           |
| 2     | cups nuts — chopped                      |
| 1     | cup dates — chopped                      |
| 2     | tablespoons vanilla                      |
| 1     | pound Canelake's Sweet Chocolate —cubed  |

Cream shortening & sugars. Add eggs one at a time. Add flour & baking powder. Put soda into boiling water then add to mixture. Add vanilla. Roll dates in flour to coat (this makes the dates separate from each other) then add along with the nuts and cubed chocolate; add all these in with spoon and mix by hand. Bake on greased sheet at 350 º or 10-12 minutes until a nice tan color. Cool on cooling racks.

- - - - - - - - - - - - - - - - -

NOTES : Mother told me that she had found this cookie recipe during the year I was born, 1939. This is another cookie which she could never leave out of her holiday baking. While reading this recipe, one will wonder where they can purchase "Canelake's Chunk O' Chocolate". The most wonderful candy store in Virginia, Minnesota was owned by the Canelake family. For 75 years, they made and are still making their own candy. Mom always bought their chunk chocolate for this cookie. If you can't get to Virginia, Minnesota to buy Canelakes's Chocolate, the large sweet chocolate blocks sold in your local super market will do just fine.

# Cheese Potica

Serving Size : 30

|     |                      |
|-----|----------------------|
| 1   | Dough                |
| 2   | pounds cottage cheese |
| 1/2 | cup butter — melted  |
| 2   | eggs — beaten        |

Use the same dough recipe as for the Apple Potica.
Use the same method for mixing and stretching the
dough.  After dough is stretched onto the floured cloth,
mix together the above ingredients and spread completely over the stretched out dough.  Use the very
same method to coil the potica into the greased pan.
You may bake the potica immediately at 350 º for 1
hour, or you may freeze until ready to use as directed in
the other recipe.

- - - - - - - - - - - - - - - - -

NOTES : I can't say enough about this recipe.  Everyone loves it. It may not sound very good, but tasting is
the true test.  Mother had to make this for all the relatives' weddings. If she didn't there would be unhappy
faces all over the room.  Our Italian cousins, the Gingerelli's, always request cheese potica for any occasion, and they usually only like Italian food. I guess,
what with my dad's Croatian background, and while
growing up,  these kids spent a lot of time at our home,
they got to enjoy his ethnic food as well.

# Cheese Ravioli

Serving Size : 8

## Filling

| | |
|---|---|
| 1/2 | pound ricotta cheese |
| 1/4 | cup parmesan cheese |
| 1/4 | teaspoon salt |

## **Dough

| | |
|---|---|
| 3 | cups flour |
| 3 | teaspoons salt |
| 3 | eggs |
| 1/2 | cup water — lukewarm |
| 1/2 | pound butter — melted Parmesan cheese — sprinkled |

Make a well in the flour. Add eggs, mix lightly with flour, then gradually knead in water until dough makes a nice smooth ball. This takes about 15 minutes by hand; if you have a dough hook it comes together into a ball much faster. Knead for a few minutes then let rest on a lightly floured surface for 20 minutes. If you have a noodle roller, it works best to roll the dough. Cut off a piece of dough, 1 inch thick, put through noodle roller then lay on floured table. With rolling pin, roll a little thinner; the strip of dough should be at least 3 inches wide, then place heaping teaspoon of filling on dough one inch apart on lower side of strip. Flap back edge of dough over filling and press down onto front edge. Cut with crimper/cutter tool, remove from table with metal spatula and lay onto floured baking sheet. Continue to make raviolis and after pan is full, place in freezer, After raviolis are frozen, you may put them into zip-lock baggies for use at any time. They freeze beautifully for

6 months.  When ready to use, place frozen ravioli into boiling water for 20 minutes, drain and cover with melted butter and sprinkle with parmesan cheese.  Do not run these under cold water as we do other spaghetti noodles because they might open and fall apart.  If you want to serve raviolis immediately after making, just keep them on floured pan until ready to use.  Prepare them in the same manner as we do for frozen ravioli.

\*\*This is a much softer dough than the meat ravioli, therefore, a little more difficult to handle when rolling, but don't be afraid, it turns out beautifully.

- - - - - - - - - - - - - - - - - -

Serving Ideas : Serving size is about 8-10 ravioli per person.

NOTES : This is better than any gourmet food you might eat in a fabulous restaurant. It is a delicacy.  Once people eat cheese ravioli, they never forget it.  Our family celebrations are never without cheese raviolis. At all of our parties we serve both the cheese and the meat raviolis, but we always run out of the cheese, it never fails.  We can't ever seem to make enough of these fabulous little pillows.  Even the little grand-children love them.  After church on Sundays, my grandchildren would come to my restaurant for breakfast, and for years, my granddaughter Kasey, who is 10, had always asked, "Can I have cheese ravioli?" and I always had to say, "Not for breakfast, honey." People love them as an hors d'oeuvre with their cocktails or wine. We often had to worry  that guests would eat so many they would loose their appetite for dinner; but it never happened.

# Cocoa Drop Cookies

Serving Size : 24

| | |
|---|---|
| 1/2 | cup butter — beaten |
| 2/3 | cup brown sugar |
| 1 | egg— beaten |
| 1/2 | cup milk |
| 1 | teaspoon vanilla |
| 2 | cups cake flour — level |
| 1/4 | teaspoon salt |
| 1 1/2 | teaspoons baking powder |
| 6 | tablespoons cocoa |

### Variation #1

| | |
|---|---|
| 1 | dozen marshmallows — halved |
| 1 | recipe Chocolate glaze |

### Variation #2

| | |
|---|---|
| 3 | cups coconut |
| 3 | cups butter frosting |
| | food coloring |

Cream together butter & sugar. Add egg, beat well. Add vanilla & milk alternately with dry ingredients.

**Variation #1**: Drop teaspoonful of dough onto greased baking sheet & bake at 350 º for 8-10 minutes. Cover with marshmallow half, return to oven for 45 seconds to set. Cool on cooling racks. When completely cooled, frost with chocolate glaze.

**Variation #2**: Drop 1/2 teaspoonful of dough onto greased baking sheet & bake for 5-7 minutes. Remove onto cooling racks. When completely cooled, press together two cookies with your butter frosting, then completely frost entire cookie which now looks like a round ball, then roll whole frosted cookie in coconut.

------------------------

NOTES : One day when mom was looking for something pretty & colorful to place on her Christmas cookie tray, she created these two variations from the plain chocolate drop cookie. As kids we always loved these even though we had to help roll the coconut variation; a messy job, easier with two people rolling, but it's worth the mess. As with all of her cookies, these two freeze very well. The coconut one is  especially good after it's been partially thawed and  still a little cold.  Tint the butter frosting red & green for Christmas, or pastels for other holidays and celebrations.  They certainly add color to any cookie tray.  If her grandson, David, was going to be around for the holidays, the chocolate/ marshmallow version was a must, or he would have been disappointed.....and good old Grandma Grace wouldn't disappoint anybody.

## Cream of Carrot Soup

Serving Size : 20

|     |                           |
| --- | ------------------------- |
| 2   | pounds carrots — shredded |
| 1   | pound butter — melted     |
| 2   | cups flour                |
| 2   | cups milk                 |
| 8   | quarts water              |
| 1/2 | cup onion flakes          |
| 1   | teaspoon white pepper     |
| 1   | teaspoon  baking soda     |
| 2   | teaspoons  salt           |
| 2   | tablespoons  parsley flakes |

Put enough water in kettle to just cover carrots. Simmer until soft.  Add onion flakes.  With the butter, flour and milk, make a white sauce.  Before adding the white sauce to the carrots, add the baking soda.  Add white sauce, salt, pepper.  Mix well then sprinkle with parsley flakes.

- - - - - - - - - - - - - - - - -

NOTES : Anytime that you add a white sauce to a soup, you must add a teaspoon of baking soda or your soup will curdle. Once soup has curdled, it is ruined.  This carrot soup is great. The first time I ever saw it, I thought it looked kind of bland like most creamed soups, but you have to try this one to believe how good it is.  Of course, don't skimp on the carrots; that's what jives it the nice robust flavor.

# Cream of Turkey Soup

Serving Size : 20

|       |                          |
|-------|--------------------------|
| 1     | turkey carcass           |
| 4     | quarts broth             |
| 1     | pound carrots — diced    |
| 6     | stalks celery — diced    |
| 1     | large onion — diced      |
| 1     | stick margarine          |
| 2     | cups rice                |
| 2     | cans peas — drained      |
|       | turkey — pieces          |
| 1     | teaspoon baking soda     |
| 2     | teaspoons salt           |
| 2     | teaspoons white pepper   |

## White Sauce

|         |                        |
|---------|------------------------|
| 4       | tablespoons margarine  |
| 1/2     | cup flour              |
| 1-1/2   | cups milk              |

Boil turkey carcass for a couple of hours then drain.
Boil rice, drain then set aside. Sauté diced vegetables
in margarine until transparent. Add vegetables and rice
to hot broth, let simmer. To make white sauce, melt the
margarine, quickly add the flour stirring constantly, then
add the milk all at once, stirring constantly. Before
adding the white sauce to the broth, be sure to add the
1 teaspoon of baking soda or your soup will curdle.
Now add the white sauce and then the peas, salt and
pepper. Add any amount of turkey scraps that have
been left over from your turkey.

- - - - - - - - - - - - - - - - - -

NOTES : After your holiday meal or any occasion for which one uses turkey, this is the best way to finish off the scraps. This soup is so delicious, you will not want it to end.  Mother made this soup for so many years, that sometimes I think we wanted to eat a turkey just so we could finally get this soup again. With grocery products being so diverse today, one can make this soup anytime by using the chicken base from a jar instead of boiling bones.  Actually, turkey bones don't have much flavor, therefore, it's always a good idea to add either a few bouillon cubes to the broth or a couple of tablespoons of chicken base.  This white sauce is a basic white sauce which may be used with any foods that call for a white sauce topping.  When adding flour and milk to make sauces, always use a wire whip to stir.  It prevents any lumps and your white sauce will be so creamy, you won't believe it. This soup is a sure hit for young and old alike, no one will complain about still eating leftovers.

# Cuduri

Serving Size : 12

| | |
|---|---|
| 8 | cups flour |
| 1/2 | teaspoon salt |
| 3 | packages yeast — dry |
| 1 | cup water — lukewarm |
| 1 | quart oil |

Mix yeast in water, set aside. Mix flour and salt. Add yeast mixture to flour mixture with hook. After it forms a soft ball, place on floured surface and knead to put together into a nice shape. Place ball in oiled bowl, cover with cloth till double in bulk. Take 1/2 cup dough and roll into a rope 1/2" wide x 8" long. Shape into a figure 8. Lay the shaped roll on a floured cookie sheet. Again, raise rolls till double. Fry raised rolls in deep fryer with the raised side down. Watch the edges till golden, then turn to other side to fry. Remove from oil and lay on paper towels to blot some of the oil. While warm, dip into sugar.

- - - - - - - - - - - - - - - - -

NOTES : Mother told me that when she was a little girl, one day she was watching her father frying Cuduri. As all the rolls cooked, he never removed the first one. Naturally, with a child's curiosity, she wondered why he left it in the pot so she asked him. Since he was an immigrant and didn't have much to say to the children, he just swung at her, as if to hit her, and said, "Aw Shut up!" She almost fell off her chair. So much for "parenting skills" that we all hear about today. The immigrants didn't know how to talk to their children and the word "psychology" was unheard of, but the children respected their parents and elders, and there weren't all the problems we hear about today with kids. I'm not a psychologist, and don't claim to be an expert so I guess I shouldn't be expounding on the subject, I'm just stating an observation.

# Dago Soup

Serving Size : 20

| | |
|---|---|
| 10 | carrots — diced |
| 5 | stalks celery — diced |
| 1 | whole onion — diced |
| 10 | quarts chicken broth |
| 1 | pound tomatoes, canned — diced |
| | juice from tomatoes |
| | salt and pepper — to taste |
| 1 | whole chicken |

## Dumplings

| | |
|---|---|
| 1/2 | cup parmesan cheese |
| 4 1/2 | cups flour |
| 10 | eggs — beaten |
| 1 | teaspoon salt |
| 1/2 | teaspoon  black pepper |
| 3 | cups bread crumbs |

In large kettle, boil chicken, strain, reserving liquid for soup.  Remove all chicken meat off the bones, save to add at end of soup.  In broth, boil celery and carrots until done, add tomatoes and juice. Mix dumplings, this mixture will be soft.  Be sure that broth is boiling then push the soft dumpling mixture through a "ricer" into the boiling broth.  Be careful for your fingers, but plunge the ricer right into the broth as it is the only way for the dumplings to come off the ricer.  Have a table knife handy to scrape the excess dough off the ricer and just put it into the broth.  It doesn't matter if the dumplings are different shapes,  the excess dough will make little

larger dumplings. Add your chicken pieces, sprinkle
with parsley.

- - - - - - - - - - - - - - - - - -

NOTES : I'm hoping that no one will take offense to the
name of this soup.  The Iron Range was such an ethnic
melting pot, and all of the different nationalities were
nick-named.  Being "politically correct" was not important, as the Rangers called each other these names in a
joking manner. This is my favorite soup.  It's worth buying a "ricer" to make the dumplings.  A ricer is a useful
kitchen tool. Instead of mashing potatoes, for a change,
you may rice potatoes to add to your favorite meal.
When mother had her restaurant, all of her customers
knew that every Thursday was "spaghetti day", and
"Dago Soup" was always the soup of the day.

# Date Filled Cookies

Serving Size  : 24

## Cookie Dough

| | |
|---|---|
| 2 1/2 | cups cake flour — sifted |
| 1/2 | teaspoon  baking powder |
| 1/2 | teaspoon salt |
| 2 1/2 | cups rolled oats — ground fine |
| 1 | cup butter |
| 1 | cup brown sugar |
| 1/2 | cup water |

## Filling

| | |
|---|---|
| 1/2 | cup  dates — chopped |
| 1/2 | cup water |
| 1 | tablespoon lemon juice |
| 1/4 | cup sugar |
| 1 | tablespoon flour |
| | salt — dash |

Cream butter with sugar until fluffy.  Mix flour, baking powder and salt with rolled oats.  Add dry ingredients alternately with water.  Chill for an hour.

While dough is chilling, mix together the date filling. Combine all ingredients and cook until thick.  Cook on low heat, stirring often.  It doesn't take long to thicken. Cool until ready to use.

On lightly floured board, roll dough about 1/8" thick.

Cut out rounds with a 3" cookie cutter. Bake on greased baking sheet in 350 º oven for about 10 minutes or until browned. Cool slightly, then heap 1 teaspoon date filling on lower half of cookie. Fold top half to completely cover bottom half, then seal by pressing a fork along the edge.

- - - - - - - - - - - - - - - - -

NOTES : This was mother's personal favorite cookie. I find it interesting that any of the goodies we make for holidays could be made at any time during the year, but we always wait and make them once a year. Perhaps that's why we look so forward to the same treats every year. The holidays never went by that mother wouldn't bring a box of date fills to my brother, Mark. Even when she was sick with her cancer, she had to bring Mark his date fills for the Christmas holidays. It's funny, I never heard Mark say that he liked this cookie; but then, if you knew my brother, Mark, you never heard him say much of anything; he is a quiet man, very much like our father. My sister Barbara,also, loves this cookie. To ensure receiving them for her holiday trays, she would always be sure to go to mom's shop and help her make them. Goodies baked with someone you love are perhaps the best treats because of the fun that goes into the sharing experience.

# Devil's Food Cake

Serving Size : 10

| | |
|---:|:---|
| 1/2 | cup shortening — level |
| 1 1/2 | cups sugar |
| 2 | eggs |
| 1 | teaspoon salt |
| 1 | teaspoon vanilla |
| 3 | tablespoons cocoa |
| 4 | drops red food coloring |
| 1 | tablespoon water |
| 1 | cup milk — soured |
| 2 | cups flour, cake — level |
| 1 | teaspoon baking soda — level |

Cream shortening and sugar well. Add salt & vanilla. Add eggs & continue beating well until smooth. Combine cocoa, red food coloring & water into a smooth paste; add to mixture. Alternate flour with soda and milk; always start & end with flour/soda mix. Mix the flour in 3 times, and the milk twice. Do not overbeat, just mix to a nice creamy texture. Bake in a 9"x13" pan, or two 9" round pans. Bake at 325 º for 35 to 40 minutes.

*For 2 layer cakes, see instructions as to removal of 'cakes from round pans. Also, see recipe for "White Fluffy Frosting".

- - - - - - - - - - - - - - - - - -

Serving Ideas : A white fluffy frosting is the best way to top this.

NOTES : This cake is the family's favorite. I had it for my wedding cake. Until my brother Barry was well into his fifties, mother made this cake for his birthday, and brought it to him no matter where he happened to be that day. This was another tradition that she couldn't let go. It was so wonderful to have a mother who always wanted to make us feel special on our birthday. After our parents are gone, we no longer are anybody's child, and no one ever again will want to bake our favorite cake. The figural cakes pictured on the next few pages, were all made from this recipe. It stays moist for a long time; however, mother rarely allowed us to eat some of these cakes. It would take her a week to bake and decorate some of them, such as the train cake for my brother Mark's second birthday.

Pictured below is my sister, Barbara on her fourth birthday. Mother loved making doll cakes. She would buy a plastic doll, wash it well, make a drape for the bodice, maybe a hat on her head, then insert it into the center of a cake and decorate the cake to look like a lady in a full dress. During the Fifties, this was quite a popular way to decorate a cake. It was considered to be so feminine, and little girls felt so special with their own little doll cake. I don't think that they were ever eaten.

My sister, Joan at age twelve, proudly standing by
her castle cake. Mom loved fussing with birthday
cakes; it made us feel so special. Mom loved to tell
this story on Joan: Joan was still a pre-schooler
when my brother Barry and I were in school. When
mother would make a cake she would tell Joan to
keep it secret and not tell us that a surprise was waiting for us after supper in the cake container which
was stored on a top shelf in the kitchen cupboard.
Joan could barely wait for me to get home from
school and she would whisper to me, "Sha', there's a
"Happy To Me" in the cupboard, and we would all
squeal with delight.

Pictured below is my brother Mark at age two with his train cake (which nobody ever ate as it sat on display for our enjoyment, and we let it get too old to eat). Mark was the baby of the five of us.

# Fattigmond

Serving Size : 48

| | |
|---|---|
| 6 | egg yolks — beaten |
| 6 | tablespoons cream |
| 6 | tablespoons sugar |
| | pinch salt |
| 2 | cups flour |
| 1 | quart oil — vegetable |

Beat together yolks and salt until very stiff, about 10 minutes. Blend in sugar and cream. Add flour all at once; mix well. Knead dough on floured surface until small bubbles appear. Divide in half, roll out pieces very thinly. Cut fattigmond pieces into strips 6" long by 2" wide; make a slit in one end and put the other end through the slit. Deep fry in hot oil until golden brown. Place onto paper towel to absorb the grease. After cooled, sprinkle with powdered sugar. Store in loose container. These cannot be frozen. Deep fried products do not freeze well Also, don't store in a tightly fitted tupperware because it causes the product to get moist. The object of fried food is to keep it crisp.

- - - - - - - - - - - - - - - - -

NOTES : Mother made fattigmonds for every holiday. She didn't seem to have any preference for which celebration these should be served. Of course, no wedding dinner would have been complete without fattigmonds. My brother, Mark, the youngest of our five siblings, loved these best. I never received fattigmonds from mother, but every holiday, she would say, "I have to bring Mark his fattigmonds".

# Fried Green Peppers in Oil

Serving Size : 6

| | |
|---|---|
| 3 | large green peppers — sliced |
| 1 | large onion — sliced |
| 2 | cups olive oil |
| 1 | teaspoon garlic — minced |
| 1 | teaspoon salt |
| 1/2 | teaspoon pepper |

In large skillet,heat olive oil but don't overheat or it will burn and smoke. Add onions and peppers to hot oil. Turn down heat to simmer.Stir frequently. Add garlic, salt & pepper. Cook until vegetables are soft,doesn't take too long, about 15 to 20 minutes.

- - - - - - - - - - - - - - - - -

NOTES : This is a wonderful side dish with any Italian dinner. Mother rarely served a complete Italian dinner without this recipe.  My father loved it. He had terrible stomach problems, but he still enjoyed the Italian food. Actually unless you add crushed red peppers to your food, Italian food isn't hot, it's spicy and tasty. Mother had a habit of filling her serving bowls right to the top. I never tend to do that because I feel that the contents will spill out, but mother's food always looked so enticing in her bowls that looked like they were about to erupt with scrumptiously delicious smelling concoctions. And she was so quick.  You could just drop in on her, and it seemed like in minutes the table was filled with food, the room was smelling of fabulous aromas,and you just stepped from the other room putting away your coat or washing your hands.

# Frosting - 3 Variations

Serving Size : 1

## Chocolate Glaze

| | |
|---|---|
| 1 | baking chocolate square |
| 1 | tablespoon butter |
| 1 1/2 | tablespoons milk — hot |
| 1/2 | cup powdered sugar |
| | dash salt |

## Confectioner's Icing

| | |
|---|---|
| 1 | cup powdered sugar |
| 1/2 | teaspoon vanilla |
| 2 | tablespoons  water |

## Butter Frosting — * see note

| | |
|---|---|
| 2 | cups powdered sugar |
| 1/2 | cup butter |
| 1 | teaspoon vanilla |
| 3 | tablespoons   milk |

Note:    to make a butter frosting chocolate, just — add 1/4 cup baking cocoa.

The method to make a frosting is to mix together all ingredients and beat to a smooth texture.  Using an electric beater is often the best way to remove all lumps from the powdered sugar.  Beating hard with a good wire whip can produce the same results.

A glaze should be a thin icing that can be poured

48

over the cookie or cake.

An icing should also be thin enough to pour over your bakery.

A butter frosting is thicker and creamier. It should be a nice soft consistency and easily spread onto bakery with a spreading spatula or a butter knife. A spreading spatula is the best way to spread on frosting. Most stores that sell kitchen aides will stock spreading knives. Mom always said that no kitchen should be without a spreading spatula for frosting; I absolutely agree with her. If you double your recipes for cookies or any bakery product, simply double your frosting recipes. Frostings are very simple to make, just be sure they're nice and spreadable. If too thin, add more powdered sugar, if too thick, add a touch more liquid. Just remember that frosting thins out very quickly, so add your liquid a little at a time.

# Gnocchi

Serving Size : 12

| | |
|---|---|
| 2 1/2 | pounds potatoes (6 large) — riced |
| 8 | cups flour |
| 1 | egg |
| 1 | teaspoon salt |
| 1 | cup parmesan cheese |

Peel then boil potatoes until tender. Press through ricer. Cool a little, but work while potatoes are warm. Add all ingredients, mix well until a nice stiff ball is formed. (Dough works best with dough hook.) Let ball rest under covered cloth for 20 minutes. Cut off 1 inch pieces of dough and roll into long ropes 1/2 inch thick. Cut rope into 1/2 inch pieces, and with your index and long fingers, make a dent into the center of dough so that it curves like a little cave. (This helps in the cooking process to cook thoroughly.) On floured baking pan, lay out all pieces of dough until ready to use. It doesn't matter if they dry out. Use up all of the dough. As all home-made pastas, gnocchi can also be prepared in advance and frozen until ready to use. After your floured tray is full of gnocchi, place in freezer. When frozen, use spatula to remove, then bag. When ready to cook, drop gnocchi in salted, boiling water, stir. When gnocchi rise to the top, remove to serving platter. Do not run under cold water, top immediately with spaghetti sauce. Sprinkle with more parmesan cheese, serve immediately.

- - - - - - - - - - - - - - - - - -

NOTES : Gnocchi is my personal favorite Italian dish. This recipe says that it will serve 12 people, however, they can't have my lust for gnocchi. One time I was at mom and dad's house for a typically wonderful Sunday dinner. I filled my plate so full of gnocchi that my dad thought I had filled a serving plate and was going to start to take food off it, I pulled away the plate and said, "That's my plate!" Needless-to-say, until the day my father died, I could never live down that incident, but....nobody has ever taken food off my plate since. Even the grandchildren love gnocchi. When serving a buffet dinner, we have to let the adults take their servings before the grand-children take theirs, or there would not be any gnocchi left for the adults. All I know is that there is something special about gnocchi, it is the Italian potato dumpling; if you like dumplings, you will love these.

# Italian Beans in Spaghetti Sauce

Serving Size : 8

 2 pounds Italian green beans — canned
 2 cups spaghetti sauce — heated

Heat the beans.  Add the spaghetti sauce into the beans.  Serve hot.

- - - - - - - - - - - - - - - - - -

Serving Ideas : Wonderful side dish to accompany a favorite meal.

NOTES : This is so simple it's hard to believe how good it is.  Years ago, mother would go through the bother of sautéing tomato paste and seasonings in oil.  One day when she was really busy, she decided to add the spaghetti sauce because actually it's the same thing; the sauce is made from the same ingredients, and has already been saute'ed.  She did this with the antipasto, green bean soup, or any dish that needed to have tomato paste sautéed in oil. I guess it's true that necessity is the mother of invention, and when you're a busy lady, raising a large family, inventive ideas had better happen. One of the reasons mother was such a good cook, is because she didn't have much time to follow exact recipes, and that's when her flair for which ingredient could be used as a substitute, or how something could be made easier, had to come to the forefront.

# Italian Dressing

Serving Size : 20

| | |
|---|---|
| 2 | cups vegetable oil |
| 2 | cups white vinegar |
| 1/2 | cup sugar |
| 2 | teaspoons salt |
| 1 1/2 | teaspoons black pepper — coarse ground |
| 1/4 | cup onion flakes — dehydrated |
| 1 | teaspoon oregano |
| 1 1/2 | teaspoons garlic — minced |

Mix together all ingredients in a quart jar. Shake well to mix. Keep refrigerated. Before serving, be sure to shake well as the oil and vinegar will have coagulated upon getting cold. In fact, about 1/2 hour before serving, take the dressing from the refrigerator so it will start to separate.

- - - - - - - - - - - - - - - - -

NOTES : When mother had her restaurant, she would sell this dressing by the quart. This is the best vinegar and oil dressing ever made. Many people told her that she should have bottled and marketed it, but she could neve be bothered doing anything but cooking.

# Italian Meatballs

Serving Size : 24

|        |                                             |
|-------:|---------------------------------------------|
| 2      | pounds beef — ground                        |
| 4      | slices bread — moistened                    |
| 1      | teaspoon salt                               |
| 1 1/2  | teaspoons black pepper — coarse ground      |
| 1      | tablespoon garlic — minced                  |
| 2      | teaspoons oregano                           |
| 1/2    | cup parmesan cheese                         |
| 2      | teaspoons parsley                           |

Soak dry bread in water for 15 minutes, then drain & squeeze out all excess water.  Mix together all ingredients.  Roll into balls.  As you roll, press the meat mixture together tightly in the palm of your hands to ensure that the ball compresses nicely and doesn't tend to fall apart.  Lay balls on baking sheet and bake at 350º  for 45 minutes.  Just before baking, pour 1/2 cup of water over the meatballs, this keeps them moist.  To avoid meatballs sticking to the pan, remove them from the pan to cool after 5 minutes.

- - - - - - - - - - - - - - - - - - - - - - - - -

Serving Ideas : Pour spaghetti sauce over the balls; serve in bowl.

NOTES : Mother always recommended serving the meatballs as suggested above because it saves sauce.  You may add the cooked meatballs to your spaghetti sauce and let it simmer for a half hour or so.  This will give both the meatballs and the sauce a very nice flavor, but the meatballs will absorb most of the sauce. If you add the balls to your sauce, be sure you have enough sauce to compensate for the couple of cups of sauce that will be absorbed into the balls. There is nothing that enhances a wonderful meal of spaghetti more than a tasty meatball. In our Italian family, we love cold meatball sandwiches on thick Italian bread. Another idea is to cut the meatballs in half, heat them, lay them on top of your Italian or French bread, lay a piece of mozzarella cheese over the balls, melt the cheese under a broiler, or microwave it, then cover the entire sandwich with heated spaghetti sauce. . . delicious!!!

# Italian Roast Beef

Serving Size : 12

| | |
|---|---|
| 10 | pounds rump roast |
| 3 | cloves garlic — minced |
| 1 | teaspoon rosemary |
| 1 | teaspoon basil |
| 1 | teaspoon oregano |
| 1/2 | cup onion — dry |
| 2 | teaspoonsblack pepper — coarse ground |
| 2 | cups water |

Assemble before bedtime the day before. Place roast in roaster. Cover with all the seasonings. Pour water around the roast. Cover with cover or aluminum foil. Cook overnight in 250 degree oven. It should cook about 8 hours. Remove from pan and save the juice. After it has cooled, slice thinly and serve with hard rolls. Use the juice for au jus with your sandwich. Before serving, re-heat the juice.

- - - - - - - - - - - - - - - - -

NOTES : When entertaining a large group for a casual party, this is a tremendous sandwich. This kind of cooking preparation certainly eliminates a lot of stress and mess on the day of your party. It is so simple, and your guests will think that you worked very hard cooking this roast. Nobody has to know. Always take compliments for your food graciously. Let everyone think that you make good cooking effortlessly. This recipe came to my rescue more times than I would like to remember.

## Italian Sausage

Serving Size : 6

| | |
|---|---|
| 1 | pound pork — ground |
| 1 | tablespoon fennel |
| 1 | tablespoon red pepper — crushed |
| 1 | teaspoon black pepper |
| 1/2 | cup water (per pound of pork) |
| | casings |

Mix together all ingredients.  Salt to taste.  Soak casings in water.

If you have a sausage machine, attach one end of the casing to the machine,  fill the hopper with sausage mix, then push through enough mixture to make the desired size sausage; tie off other end.  If you do not have a sausage machine, shape mixture into patties.  You may fry them immediately, or lay out flat on a baking sheet, freeze, then layer with sheets of waxed paper in covered container until ready to use.

When increasing amounts for more recipes, be sure to add 1/2 cup of water for each pound of meat in order to keep sausage moist.  Without adding water, any kind of ground meat in sausage, meatballs, or meatloaf will be dry, however, if you have used bread soaked in water as a bulking agent, then you have added moisture

- - - - - - - - - - - - - - - - -

NOTES : Mother grew up knowing how to make sausage.  They raised their own pigs at 101 Kimberly Avenue in Eveleth, Minnesota.  Not only pigs, but chickens and fields of gardens.  She told me that they used to rent blocks of land on Fayal Road for their potato gardens, and the worst job in the world was picking potato bugs off the potato plants.  They were raised during the depression with little money, but there was never a lack of food. Sometimes that's why I think that food was so important to her. She said that her mother was so concerned about all of the poor kids in the block that they constantly baked and cooked then brought food to all the families that didn't have such wonderful gardens as they. Because of their gardens, they felt that they were richer than the average person. Italians are wonderful farmers; they love to plant, harvest, and share their bounty with others.

# Jingle Bell Cookies

Serving Size : 48

| | |
|---|---|
| 1 | cup butter |
| 2 | eggs — beaten |
| 1 1/2 | cups brown sugar |
| 2 1/2 | cups flour |
| 4 | slices candied pineapple |
| 1/2 | pound red candied cherries — halved |
| 1 | teaspoon baking soda |
| | pinch salt |
| 1 1/2 | pounds dates — halved |
| 1 | cup filberts — whole |
| 1 | cup pecans — halved |
| 1 | cup walnuts — halved |

Cream butter and sugar, add well beaten eggs, and vanilla. Mix dry ingredients. them add fruits and nuts. Dough is so thick, you may have to mix with your hands. There is no liquid other than the beaten eggs in this recipe. Drop by tablespoon onto greased cookie sheet. Bake at 325 º for 20 minutes.

- -- - - - - - - - - - - - - - -

NOTES : Mother loved this cookie so much, but she would only make them during the holidays. Perhaps, because the name is synonymous with the Christmas. Or, perhaps, because they are so loaded with calories and fats that she dared not make them more than once a year. But when she did make them, she would carry them around in her apron pocket and munch on them all day long. They are fabulously good, but a little too rich for me.

## Jubilee Jumbos

Serving Size : 18

|       |                                |
|-------|--------------------------------|
| 1/2   | cup shortening — level         |
| 1     | cup brown sugar — packed       |
| 1/2   | cup sugar                      |
| 2     | eggs                           |
| 1     | cup evaporated milk            |
| 1     | teaspoon vanilla               |
| 2 3/4 | cups flour                     |
| 1/2   | teaspoon  baking soda          |
| 1     | teaspoon salt                  |
| 1     | cup nuts, optional — chopped   |

Cream together shortening and sugars until light and fluffy.  Add eggs and beat well.  Stir in milk and vanilla. Add dry ingredients.  Add nuts and blend thoroughly. Drop heaping tablespoons of dough onto greased baking sheet, about 2 inches apart (leaving room to spread).  Bake at 375 º for 10 minutes.  Cool on racks. When cool, frost.

Frosting:  Heat 2 tablespoons butter until golden brown,  Beat in 2 cups powdered sugar and 1/4 cup evaporated milk.  Beat until smooth.  Frost with a generous amount of frosting on cool cookie.

- - - - - - - - - - - - - - - - -

NOTES : This is a true family favorite cookie.  Much too large to serve at our weddings and holidays when a small cookie is required. Somehow, if this cookie is made smaller, it looses something. I guess it's the fact that it's called "jumbo", and that's what we expect. When this cookie is finished and put on a plate, you will never see a plate empty as quickly, with everyone saying, "Oh boy, Jubilee Jumbos." My kids, Jackie and David would have driven from Ely to Virginia any time they knew these cookies would be at Grandma's house.

# Lamb Cake

Serving Size : 15

          2    cups cake flour — sifted
          3    teaspoons baking powder
        1/4    teaspoon salt
        1/2    cup butter — creamed
      1 1/8    cups sugar
          2    egg — beaten
          1    teaspoon vanilla
        3/4    cup milk

Heat oven to 375 º.  Grease pans well and then flour.
Mix flour (which has been sifted and then spooned into
cup for measuring) baking powder, and salt. Sift together 3 times. Cream butter, add sugar a small amount
at a time, and continue creaming until mixture is light
and fluffy. Add beaten eggs and vanilla. Add flour and
milk alternately. Be sure to mix lightly and keep the batter smooth. Pour batter into face half of the mold. Fill to
the top being careful  to get batter into nose and ears.
Left over batter may be baked as cupcakes. Place back
half of mold on the top—bake face down—place on tray
and bake from 40 to 45 minutes. Remove from oven after 40 minutes and gently remove back half to test. If
done replace back half and allow to stand for 5 minutes
before removing the cake. If not done, replace back half
and return to oven for 5 minutes. When removing cake
from molds remove back half first and then front half,
carefully. Allow cake to cool - standing erect. In all our
testing and use there was no leakage of batter— no
breakage of the nose or ears and the cake was removed easily. When the cake is cool—ice with "White

Fluffy Frosting",(Gracie's "White Fluffy Frosting" will be on another page in this book) cover with coconut if desired— use 2 raisins for the eyes and a small piece of cherry for the mouth.

- - - - - - - - - - - - - - - - -

Serving Ideas : Display on pedestal cake dish.

NOTES : Wonderful cake for baby shower, first birthday, baptism, First Communion, or Easter. For Easter, you can color 1 cup coconut green with food coloring, let it dry for a while on waxed paper, then arrange the green coconut around the base of the lamb to look like a bed of grass. Use a black jelly bean for the nose, and sprinkle jelly beans in the grass.

My brother Barry's first birthday finds us sitting outside on the steps leading to our apartment in Virginia
when we lived upstairs of our Aunt Mary's. He's holding the lamb cake that became a tradition for our
family birthday parties. We are pictured with Aunt
Mary who helped mother with all her cakes. Mary
was the oldest sister in the family and mother always
had told me that Mary was her mentor in cooking. In
those days, it seems as though after marriage, families would continue to live within the same building.
The large, old homes sometimes had multiple apart-
ments, which were often used as boarding houses.

# Lettuce Prep

Serving Size : 8

| | |
|---|---|
| 1 | head lettuce |
| 2 | quarts water — cold |
| 1 | quart  ice cubes |

Remove outer leaves. To remove the heavy core from the head, grasp it firmly and bang it on the counter; it will pull right out.  Break up the whole head with your fingers.  Do not use a knife to cut lettuce as it will turn the lettuce brown where the knife touched it.  Soak the torn apart head in a large bowl with water and ice cubes for at least 1/2 hour.  Drain well in colander.  Bag then refrigerate until ready to use.

- - - - - - - - - - - - - - - - -

NOTES : Nothing is worse than eating a salad that is limp and soggy.  This is the only way to prepare your lettuce for a wonderful cold crunchy salad.  If you don't use all of the lettuce for salad, it will stay nice and fresh in a zip-lock baggie.  After you unload your groceries, it is wise to treat your lettuce in this manner, then it is ready whenever you need it.  In fact, if you use romaine lettuce, endive or parsley for garnishing, use this method to prep it.  Your garnish will be nice and crisp. If you need it right away, dry your leaves with a paper towel.  When I was a child we drove to Duluth quite often to have Sunday dinner with mother's brother Joe and his family.  He was married to a nice Italian lady named Irene Janetta Gingerelli from 11th Avenue West in Duluth.  Whenever we went to their house, there was a huge bowl of lettuce soaking in the kitchen sink, and I could already taste the nice cold salad.

# Macaroni with Baccal'a

Serving Size : 8

## Basic Macaroni Dough

| | |
|---|---|
| 4 | cups flour |
| 1 | teaspoon salt |
| 4 | eggs |
| 6 | tablespoons  water — cold |

## Baccal'a

| | |
|---|---|
| 1/2 | cup olive oil |
| 1/4 | cup butter |
| 3/4 | cup walnuts — coarsely chopped |
| 3 | tablespoons parsley — chopped |
| 1 | garlic clove — minced |
| 1 | pound cod fillet — cubed |
| 1/2 | cup parmesan cheese — grated |

In large bowl, mix flour and salt.  Make a well in center,
add eggs and water.  Mix together to form stiff dough.
(If your mixer has a dough hook, that is perfect.  Other-
wise there are so many pasta machines out there today
to eliminate mixing by hand.)  Turn dough onto lightly
floured surface and knead for a few minutes.  Cover
with cloth and let rest for 15 minutes. (Under "Pasta"
you will see various ways to handle this dough, but for
this particular recipe, you will make the dough into rope-
like pieces.)  Slice off 1" piece of dough, roll into a rope
about 3/4 " wide.  Cut into 2" pieces; place pieces on
floured pan.  Into your pot which you are going to boil
the pasta, add 2 teaspoons salt and 1 tablespoon oil to

your water. While your kettle of water is heating to boil, in another pot boil the cod for 5 minutes or until tender. Place macaroni pieces into boiling water and cook for 7 - 10 minutes or until done. Drain; set aside. ( In order to prevent pasta from sticking, stir in a little olive oil plain or butter.) Heat butter in oil over medium heat. Add nuts, parsley and garlic. Sauté for 3-4 minutes, stirring constantly. Toss together macaroni, cod, and nut mixture. Top with grated cheese. Serve immediately.

- - - - - - - - - - - - - - - - - -

NOTES : Christmas Eve was always a wonderful celebration in our home. Partly because it was also my birthday. Mother would invite all the relatives in for dinner which would start around 7:00 P.M. and last until we all would leave for Midnight Mass. Baccal'a was a "must" for this celebration, and only this celebration. In 1961, mother's brother Albert was coming home for Easter. Her sister Peenie had told her that they should make baccal'a for his homecoming. Mother was against making it for any occasion other than Christmas, but agreed to make it. Shortly after Easter, another brother, Joe, age 37, died from a sudden heart attack. After years had gone by, mother still blamed herself for making the bacca'la on Easter. She was such a superstitious woman. For rest of her life she grieved for her brother, and, needless to say,she stopped making baccal'a for Christmas. I don't mean to be maudlin; but this story was important to her life. Please try this recipe, you won't be disappointed.

Pictured below are the two brothers whom my mother adored. Albert is on the left, Joe is on the right. After Joe's death, his family remained very close to our family; we continued to celebrate holidays together. Even though Albert lived on the West Coast, their bond for each other was always very strong. Family is very important to Italians.

# Meat/Spinach Ravioli

Serving Size : 12

## Filling

| | |
|---|---|
| 30 | ounces spinach — chopped |
| 3 | pounds pork roast — ground |
| 3 | pounds beef roast — ground |
| 2 | tablespoons minced garlic |
| 2 | teaspoons black pepper — coarse ground |
| 2 | teaspoons oregano |
| 2 | teaspoons salt |
| 1 | cup parmesan cheese |

## Dough

| | |
|---|---|
| 8 | cups flour |
| 13 | eggs |
| 1 | teaspoon salt |

Season the roasts, cover with foil, then bake at 350 º for 2 hours. Save the juice in the pan and bone & grind the roasts, add juice to the ground meat along with the chopped spinach and cheese. Mix together to make a nice filling.  Mix all dough ingredients at once to form a stiff ball. ( a dough hook makes the best dough). On a floured surface, knead a little to bring the ball together. Let dough rest under a covered cloth for 20 minutes.  If you have a noodle roller it works best to roll the dough thin enough.  Cut off piece of dough, 1 inch thick, put through noodle roller, twice if necessary, then lay on floured table. With rolling pin, roll a little thinner, the strip of dough should be at least 3 inches wide,  then place heaping teaspoon of filling on dough one inch apart on lower side of strip.  Flap back edge of dough over filling and press down onto front edge.  Cut with crimper/cutter tool, remove from table with metal spatula and lay onto floured baking sheet pan. Continue to make raviolis and after pan is full, place in freezer. After raviolis are frozen, you may put them into ziplock baggies for use at any time. They freeze beautifully for 6 months. When ready to use, place frozen ravioli into boiling water for 20 minutes, drain and cover with our spaghetti sauce. Do not run these under cold water as we do other spaghetti noodles because they might open and fall apart. If you want to serve raviolis immediately after making just keep them on floured pan until ready to use. Prepare them in the same manner as we do for frozen ravioli.

- - - - - - - - - - - - - - - - -

Serving Ideas : Serving size about 5-6 ravioli per person.

NOTES : Ravioli is a family favorite. We could never have a celebration without raviolis. Even our friends who are not Italian love our ravioli. I know our guests come to our parties just to eat ravioli. Guests at our parties always know just what to expect for dinner. My daughter,Jackie, was married 14 years ago to a fellow from another area so we had some guests at the wedding who didn't know anything about us and and our family traditions. I had an Italian Festival for their reception; my son-in-law tells me that his friends still talk about the food at their wedding reception. It's fun to know that our food is memorable. But, I guess I'm that way too, I'll always remember a special occasion by the food. The best times remembered always include the best food memories, as Italians love good food wherever we go.

## STEPS IN MAKING RAVIOLI

Step 1.       Ball of Ravioli dough resting.

Step 2.       1" piece of dough cut from ball.

Step 3.       Rolling dough thru the noodle
              machine to make it thinner.

Step 4.       The rolled out dough with
              tablespoonsfull of meat filling.

Step 5.       Strip being cut into individual ravioli.

Step 6.       Ravoli laid out on tray ready to
              cook  or  freeze.

Step 1

Step 2.

Step 3.

Step 4.

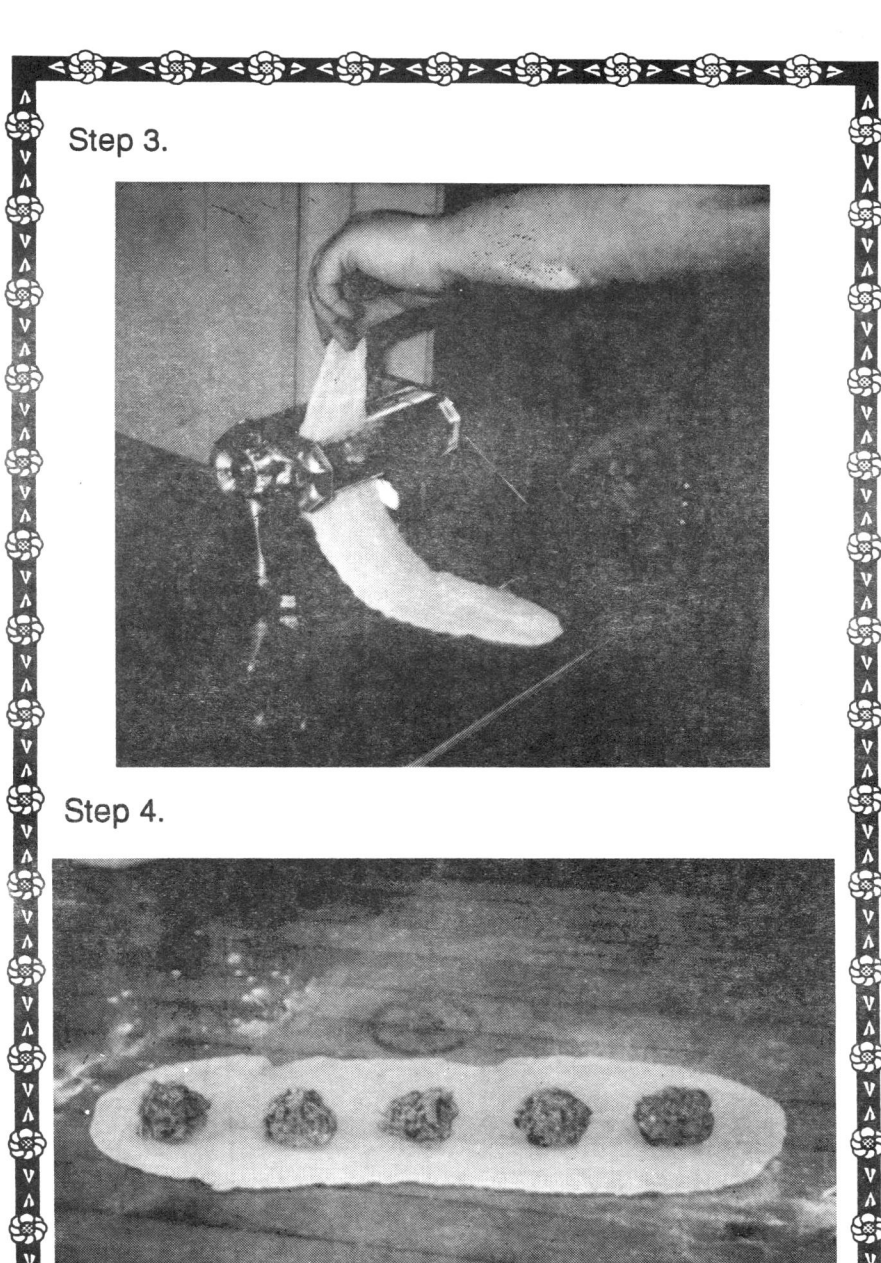

Step 5.

Step 6.

# Mint Topped Brownies

Serving Size : 10

| | |
|---|---|
| 1/4 | cup butter |
| 1 | cup sugar |
| 2 | eggs |
| 2 | baking chocolate squares — melted |
| 1/4 | cup milk |
| 2/3 | cup flour |
| 1/2 | teaspoon baking powder |
| 1/8 | teaspoon salt |
| 1 | teaspoon vanilla |
| 1 | cup nuts — chopped |

## Mint Topping

| | |
|---|---|
| 1 1/2 | cups powdered sugar |
| 1/8 | cup cream |
| 1 | tablespoon butter |
| 1/4 | teaspoon peppermint extract |

## Chocolate Glaze**

| | |
|---|---|
| 1 | baking chocolate square |
| 1 | tablespoon butter |
| 1 1/2 | tablespoons milk — hot |
| 1/2 | cup powdered sugar |
| | dash salt |

This is a 3 step process. Cream together sugar & butter, add eggs and vanilla and beat well. Add chocolate. Alternate flour & baking powder with milk then add nuts. Bake at 350 º for 20-25 minutes in 8" square greased and floured pan. Topping: Combine powdered sugar & cream in sauce pan. Cook over direct heat until it reaches a soft ball. Remove and add butter, cool to lukewarm. Add flavoring then beat until thick and creamy.  Spread over baked, cooled bars. Glaze: Melt chocolate and butter over hot water. Combine milk, sugar, & salt. Add chocolate mixture gradually, blending well.  While warm, spread on top of mint topping.

**This glaze is great for Boston Cream Pie, cream puffs, eclairs, or anything that just needs a light glaze rather than a heavy frosting.

- - - - - - - - - - - - - - - - - -

NOTES : If you like the combination of chocolate and mint, this one is a real winner.  It is mouth wateringly good. The mint topping is so wonderful, it tastes like candy.  Mom put together this scrumptious bar from 3 different recipes.  When I was a kid, I had to beat the mint topping in cold water in the bathroom sink, and always grumbled while I was doing it, but the effort was worth it as I ate my fair share.  Sometimes while we're cooking and nobody wants to help, I'm always reminded of the story of "The Little Red Hen". She did all of the work and when it was over, all the little chicks wanted to get in on the fun at the end.  That's how I used to feel when I was at that sink beating the mint topping.

## Mocha Balls

Serving Size : 24

| | |
|---|---|
| 3 | eggs — beaten |
| 1 | cup sugar |
| 1 | cup flour |
| 1 | teaspoon vanilla |
| 3 | tablespoons water |
| 1 | teaspoon baking powder |
| 2 | packages salted Spanish peanuts — ground |

Pre-heat oven to 350 º.  Bake for 25 to 30 minutes.

Mix in order to a nice smooth batter.  Grease & flour bottom of 8" x 8" square pan.  Cool completely.  Cut into 1"x1" squares.  Frost on all 4 sides with  butter frosting listed in this book. Frost one at a time, and immediately roll each ball in ground salted Spanish peanuts.  Set on waxed paper to dry.  After frosting & nuts have set, pack away in airtight container.  May be frozen. (See instructions for freezing ).

- - - - - - - - - - - - - - - - - -

NOTES : For some reason these are little square cakes and we have always called them "balls".  Perhaps it's because after they are completed they look like little balls.  This is one item our family could never be without on a holiday.  In fact, living with a very superstitious mother, Christmas could never go by without making "Mocha Balls".  Mother always made these

with a lady friend who would help her frost & roll.  One
year, the lady friend wasn't available to help so mother
made them herself.  The following year, the lady friend
developed cancer and my mother never forgave herself
for breaking a tradition.  In my mother's world, you
never broke a tradition or bad luck would befall you. I'm
sure that superstition came with her mother from Italy.
So, every  year, mother had to make mocha balls to
prevent any bad luck from happening to her or someone
she loved.

Pictured below is Gracie at a very young age with one of her favorite nieces, Lois Baumgartner Mattei, who was about two years old.  Her mother, Rosie, was mother's older sister.  Mother told me that Rosie is the one who found the mocha ball recipe. One day she called mother to come to her house and bake this new recipe with her.  The sisters used to bake together quite a bit.  Lois always stayed close to her Auntie Gracie, and as she got older, every  Christmas she would go to the shop and help mother make the mocha balls.  Even the last Christmas, when mother was very ill, Lois made mocha balls with her.

# Oatmeal Bread

Serving Size : 2

| | |
|---|---|
| 1 | cup rolled oats |
| 2 | cups boiling water |
| 1/3 | cup molasses |
| 1 | tablespoon shortening |
| 2 | packets yeast |
| 1/4 | cup water — lukewarm |
| 1 | teaspoon salt |
| 4 | cups flour |

Place oatmeal in large mixing bowl, add boiling water, molasses and shortening. Let cool until just warm. Dissolve yeast in lukewarm water and let rise. After water mixture has cooled, add yeast that has risen, then add flour and salt. Mix with dough hook to form a soft ball, or knead by hand until the dough feels soft yet firm. Shape into a ball. Place in greased bowl, cover with clothe and set in warm place until double in bulk. Divide the dough into two pieces and shape into loaves. Place in greased loaf pans, prick with a fork to release all air bubbles, cover with cloth till double in bulk then bake in 375 º oven for 45 to 50 minutes until golden brown. Remove from pans immediately after baking then cool on cooling racks.

- - - - - - - - - - - - - - - -

NOTES : This bread freezes beautifully. If you want to increase the recipe size to make more than two loaves, please do. Baking bread is a lot of work so sometimes it's nice to make a large batch to freeze and have it on hand for a while. Once you start to bake your own bread, store bought bread will never do. Your family will get hooked on it. When mother had her restaurant, she had a customer who insisted she make bread for him whenever his freezer ran out. She would make him 12 loaves at one time. Even if it were inconvenient for her to bake bread on a day that he would come in and ask her, she could never say "no" to anybody, so she would fit it into her busy schedule and before she left her shop, his fresh bread would be sitting on the racks, cooling, waiting to be picked up. Needless to say, he thought that she was "better than sliced bread".

# Oranges Ala Oil

Serving Size : 8

### Variation No. 1
| | |
|---|---|
| 4 | oranges — large |
| 2 | tablespoons olive oil |
| 1/2 | teaspoon salt |
| 1/2 | teaspoon pepper |

### Variation No. 2
| | |
|---|---|
| 2 | tablespoons powdered sugar |

Slice oranges and lay on round tray in a circular manner.

For Variation No. 1, drizzle oil on top of oranges then sprinkle with salt and pepper. The salt and pepper will run off the oranges if it is put on first. When added last, they will adhere better.

For Variation No. 2, sprinkle powdered sugar over oranges then enjoy.

- - - - - - - - - - - - - - - - - -

NOTES : This is a must at all Italian buffets. Mother always told me that the adults like the oranges with the oil, and the children like the oranges with powdered sugar. It's a good way to get kids to eat fruit. The little bit of powdered sugar certainly won't harm them.

# Palm Bread

Serving Size : 24

| | |
|---|---|
| 2 | cups water — warm |
| 2 | packets yeast — dry |
| 1 | teaspoon salt |
| 1/2 | cup sugar |
| 1/4 | cup oil |
| 1 | egg — beaten |
| 2 | tablespoons anise seed |
| 7 | cups flour |
| 6 | eggs — raw |
| 1 | palm — fresh |

Dissolve yeast salt and sugar in warm water. After this mixture has cooled, add oil and beaten egg. Add flour and anise seed.Mix together and knead till a soft yet firm ball takes shape. Put into greased bowl; let rise till double. Now for the fun part....divide the dough into two parts, shape into balls. Divide each ball into three pieces. Roll each piece into a long strip, approximately one and one half inches wide by twelve inches long. On your greased baking pan, braid the three strips. As you braid, place a raw egg between the braid at three different points. Push the egg right down into the dough . At the top of the braid, place a palm cross at the top of the first egg. Cover & let rise again. Bake at 350 º for 30 to 40 minutes or until golden brown. Remove from pan to cooling racks. When slicing the bread, the eggs are now cooked, and can be eaten. This bread is also delicious toasted.

Freezes well.

- - - - - - - - - - - - - - - - - -

NOTES : In order to get the palms, you must go to church on Palm Sunday. This is usually made on Good Friday. While you're waiting for your bread to rise, cut your palm into pieces about 4"x4", put two slits into two of the pieces then weave the other pieces through to form a cross.  Mother was a very superstitious person. She believed that one never broke a tradition, for if you did, bad luck would befall you.  In all of her adult life, she never failed to make her Easter Bread.  One year at Easter time, she was very ill. She called me crying because she was too ill to make her bread, therefore, she was sure that someone would die if she broke the tradition and didn't make the bread that year.  The next day, I rushed to her home to make her bread. After I arrived, she felt a little more motivated and started showing me what to do.  By the time I brought out all the necessary pots, pans & cut the palms into crosses, she had the Easter bread raising in a bowl. Nobody she knew died that year.

# Pasty

Serving Size : 12

| | |
|---|---|
| 5 | pounds potatoes — peeled & diced |
| 1 | pound carrots — peeled & diced |
| 1 | small rutabaga — optional |
| | butter |
| 2 | teaspoons salt |
| 1 | teaspoon black pepper |
| 1 1/2 | pounds beef — ground |
| 1 | small onion — diced |

## Crust

| | |
|---|---|
| 7 | cups flour |
| 1 | pound lard |
| 1 1/2 | teaspoons salt |
| 1 1/8 | cups  water — cold |
| 1 | tablespoon vinegar |

Mix diced vegetables with ground beef,salt and pepper.

**Crust:** Cut lard into flour and salt. Add water & vinegar all at once, (just like pie crust) and mix quickly to form nice ball. Do not overbeat pasty or pie dough as it will become tough. On floured table, roll out 1/2 cup of dough into 8" circle. Put 1 cup of meat filling on lower 1/3 portion of rolled dough, add 1 tablespoon butter on top, then fold top of dough over meat filling & butter. Push together tightly the top & bottom crusts, then crimp excess dough into a nice fluted edge.  The end result should have a half moon look pasty pie. To allow air to escape while baking, slice a small hole in top crust, then brush top with milk to seal edge of pasty. Bake on floured sheet pan at 350 º for 45 min. to 1 hour or until pasty is a nice golden brown. To ensure a nice flaky crust, cooling process is very important. Remove from pan immediately and place on cooling racks. Pasties freeze very nicely. Be sure they are completely cooled before freezing. Microwave heating is not recommended, however, if necessary, may be-plain zapped 4-5 minutes when thawed, or 8-10 minutes when frozen. To heat in a conventional oven, preheat to 350 º, then heat for about 20-25 minutes. If you would like to do this for a company dinner, prepare everything a day ahead. This pasty crust stays beautifully in the refrigerator for at least a week. If you prepare the veggies ahead, be sure to buy a produce whitener and process them so the potatoes don't turn black. Put it all in the refrigerator then be prepared to make and bake your pasties when you have time and are ready.

- - - - - - - - - - - - - - - - -

Serving Ideas : Cole slaw and gravy go well with pasty.

NOTES : This is a meat pie of Cornish descent. We grew up in mining country where a lot of immigrant miners from England settled. They brought over the "pasty". It's wonderful because it's a complete meal under a flaky crust. The miner's had a certain type of lunch box in which they carried their pasty to work; the bottom held a hot beverage which kept the pasty on top of a tin shelf above it warm till time to eat. Mother was born to be an entrepreneur. When they were young housewives, trying to earn extra money, she and her two sisters, Peenie and Rosie made pasties to sell to the public. They would make four hundred every week-end and sell them for 25 cents out of their brother Joe's Hamburger Stand in Eveleth. In those days, everyone worked so hard for very little money, but she told me that 25 cents was a lot of money at the time.

Pictured below is the building called , "The Hamburger Stand" from which mother and her sisters sold their pasties. They made wonderful hamburgers, and coneys, and it was a Taxi Stand. I can't imagine a small town like Eveleth, Mn. ever in need of a taxi service, but I guess during the forties there was.

# Pea Soup

Serving Size : 15

| | |
|---|---|
| 6 | potatoes — diced |
| 5 | carrots — diced |
| 1 | small onion — diced |
| 1 | bag split green peas |
| | ham bones |
| | ham cubes |
| 1 | teaspoon pepper |
| 2 | tablespoons ketsup |

Boil ham bone, drain for broth.  Add vegetables and peas then simmer until soft and mushy.  Stir once in a while.  This takes about 2 hours, so be sure to keep the burner on low so as not to scorch the bottom. Add the ham chunks, pepper and ketsup.

- - - - - - - - - - - - - - - -

NOTES : Mother told me that after the first time she made this recipe, my father and she immediately left for a trip to Duluth.  He couldn't stop talking about this pea soup all the way to Duluth, and could barely wait to get back home to have some more.  It's strange the way food affects people.  Perhaps at one time, it was our homemade foods that endeared a certain occasion to us for some reason or another.  Now adays, we seem to remember a wonderful food with a vacation, a favorite restaurant, or maybe sitting at a favorite outdoor cafe watching the sun set.

# Porcupine Meatballs

Serving Size : 12

| | |
|---|---|
| 1/2 | pound pork — ground |
| 1 | pound beef — ground |
| 1/4 | cup onion — chopped |
| 1/4 | cup rice — uncooked |
| 1/2 | teaspoon baking powder |
| 1/2 | teaspoon pepper |
| 1/2 | teaspoon salt |
| 1 | small tomato sauce |
| 1/4 | cup ketchup |

Mix together all ingredients.  Shape into meatballs. Lay all meatballs in casserole dish.  Mix together tomato sauce and ketsup, add 1/4 cup water to thin.   Pour over meatballs.  Cook at 350 º for 1 1/2 hours.  The long cooking time is due to the fact that the rice is put in raw.  The baking powder makes the meatballs puff up,and the rice pokes through, giving it the name "porcupine".

- - - - - - - - - - - - - - - - -

NOTES : Use the tomato sauce as a gravy over your potatoes.  It is surprisingly tasty. Kids as well as adults love this meatball.

# Potato/Green Bean Soup

Serving Size : 10

| | |
|---|---|
| 4 | quarts water |
| 2 | pounds green beans, canned |
| 1 | pound potatoes — cubed |
| 2 | cups spaghetti sauce |
| 2 | teaspoons salt |
| 1 | bay leaf |

In a kettle, add salt to water. Cook the potatoes until done.  Add the green beans and spaghetti sauce.  Add pepper and bay leaf.  Simmer for about 1/2 hour.  Before serving, remove the bay leaf. Mother always told me that you must remove the bay leaf because someone could choke on it.

- - - - - - - - - - - - - - - - - -

Serving Ideas : Fresh homemade bread is dynamite with this soup.

NOTES : Being Catholic meant abstaining from meat on Friday or certain church holidays.  This is the one soup that sticks out in my mind as a favorite meatless meal.  It doesn't sound very good or interesting, but I guarantee you that it passes the taste test. Even though we no longer abstain, I continue to make this; even the little kids like it because they can see what's in it. Kids are suspicious of eating anything they can't recognize; they want to know what they're eating.  I can't say that I blame them for that.  When we're in another part of the country and order unfamiliar food, I, too, am suspicious of the food that's staring at me from my plate.

# Removal of Cakes from Round Pans

Serving Size : 1

    2 or 3 layer cakes like German Sweet chocolate or rectangular cakes for all around decorating.

Grease bottom of pans only, not the sides. Put your pan on top of sheets of waxed paper and with a pencil draw the outline of the pan. Lift pan off the waxed paper then cut out the circled area with a scissors. Lay the circle on the bottom of pan, grease the waxed circle, then dust it with flour. Turn the pan upside down then "bang" on the back of it to remove excess flour. Pour cake into pan then bang the pan on the counter to remove air bubbles that may be in the batter from beating. For even cooking, always place cake pans on center rack of oven and never open the oven door while a cake is baking, or until it is 3/4 through the bake time. After baking is complete, cool your cake on cooling racks for 10 to 15 minutes. Take one cooling rack and place it on top side of cake, turn the cake upside down so it falls onto the cooling rack. Gently lift the waxed paper off the bottom of cake. Then place another cooling rack on bottom of cake and turn the cake right side up. Before frosting, let all layers of cake cool completely. When frosting chocolate cake, put a thin layer of frosting all around to hold the crumbs in place, then proceed with the rest of the frosting job.

The same method would be used for a rectangular pan, and if your cake is too long, put together two cooling racks for removal.

# Sarma, Cabbage Rolls

Serving Size : 12

| | |
|---|---|
| 1 | pound beef — ground |
| 1 | pound pork — ground |
| 1 | cup rice — cooked |
| 1 | tablespoon garlic — minced |
| 2 | teaspoons salt |
| 1 | teaspoon pepper |
| 1 | large cabbage head — frozen/wilted |
| 2 | ounces salt pork — sliced |
| 12 | ounces tomato juice |
| 16 | ounces sauerkraut |

A few days ahead of preparation, put your cabbage head in the freezer to wilt (this eliminates boiling the head to soften). Mix together the 2 meats, rice, garlic, salt, & pepper. Peel a leaf off the head and lay flat. remove some of the thickness on the outside spine of the leaf. Place 1 cup of meat mixture in lower curved end of leaf. As you roll the mixture, envelope close the 2 sides so that the mixture does not fall out while baking. Lay half of the sauerkraut on bottom of 9"x13" baking pan. Place the cabbage rolls in rows. When finished, top with rest of sauerkraut & salt pork, then pour tomato juice over entire pan. Fill pan almost to top with water. To ensure doneness of the pork, bake at 350 º for 1 1/2 - 2 hours.

- - - - - - - - - - - - - - - - -

NOTES : My father made his own sauerkraut. Every winter for years, he would have this huge crock with a wooden lid and a large boulder holding the lid tightly in place, in a corner of our basement. People probably had basements so those terrible odors of storing foods didn't have to be in the house where everyone slept and lived.  There rarely was a reason for a child to go into the basement; nothing was there except for hard work, a wringer washing machine, a coal bin, wood stacked, and all kinds of ugly looking food preserves in blue jars staring at us from the shelves.  And the belching noises from the old furnaces with the arms reaching out in all directions, like a huge monster,made children want to stay far away from all of those scary noises and sights. But I could barely wait until he would open that lid off the crock and we could start eating the sauerkraut.  I have never tasted sauerkraut from any store or deli that can even come close to matching the flavor of my father's.

# Sauerkraut and Beans

Serving Size : 20

| | |
|---|---|
| 16 | ounces pinto beans |
| 16 | ounces sauerkraut |
| 1/4 | cup flour |
| 2 | tablespoons lard |
| 1/2 | cup onion — diced |
| 1 | teaspoon pepper |

Rinse & clean pinto beans.  Boil beans until soft. Keep enough water in pan to level with beans. Add sauerkraut to beans. Make a rue with the lard and flour and add onions.  Slowly add rue to bean mixture, stirring well then add pepper. Eat and enjoy.

- - - - - - - - - - - - - - - -

NOTES : Our father enjoyed this dish so much.  My mother had to make some of the ethnic foods with which he grew up.  At first we kids thought that  this looked "icky" and it took us years to even try it. Whenever mom made this she had to bring a bowl full to Mark and Joan, and they would open the lid of the Tupperware and say, "Oh boy, sauerkraut & beans", and their children would say, "Oh, icky".  Mother always said, "What goes around comes around".

# Soft Maple Date Cookie

Serving Size : 24

| | |
|---|---|
| 1 | Cup butter |
| 1 1/2 | Cups brown sugar — packed |
| 1 | teaspoon baking powder |
| 1 | teaspoon vanilla |
| 2 | teaspoons mapeline |
| 4 | eggs |
| 3 | Cups flour |
| 1 | teaspoon baking soda |
| 1/2 cup | hot water |
| 1 | cup walnuts — chopped |
| 1 1/2 | cups dates — chopped |

Cream together butter and brown sugar. Add eggs, vanilla, and mapeline then beat well. Mix soda into hot water. Alternate baking powder & flour with hot water mixture. Stir in walnuts and dates. Bake on ungreased baking sheet at 350 º for 10 minutes or until a nice tan color.

- - - - - - - - - - - - - - - - -

NOTES : This recipe is very old. Mom had it for at least 50 years. This cookie tastes better than it looks. It may be the last one you would reach for on a cookie tray, but once you've had one, you have to have another. The mapeline flavor gives this cookie an unusual taste.

# South Americans

Serving Size : 16

|   |   |
|---|---|
| 1 | pound green serrano chili peppers — ground |
| 1 | pound red peppers — ground |
| 1 | pound onions — ground |
| 1 | pound celery — ground |
| 1 | pound beef — ground |
| 1 | pound pork — ground |
| 1 | pound canned mushrooms — ground |
| 8 | ounces tomato paste |
| 1 | pound pepperoni sausage — ground |
| 2 | cups oil |

Sauté peppers, onions and celery in the oil until transparent. In another pot, cook the beef and pork until done. Mix together all the ingredients and put into a pot. Cook in the oven for 1 hour to allow the flavors to meld together.

- - - - - - - - - - - - - - - - -

NOTES : This is like a "Sloppy Joe" except it's very hot. Eat between a bun or your favorite coarse bread. Men seem to like this sandwich with beer. When mother had her restaurant, she had standing orders to make them for the local taverns.

## Spaghetti Sauce

Serving Size : 10

|       |                                          |
|-------|------------------------------------------|
| 3     | ounce can tomato paste                   |
| 3     | pound cans tomato puree                  |
| 1/8   | cup sugar                                |
| 1     | onion — diced                            |
| 2 1/8 | teaspoons oregano                        |
| 2 1/8 | teaspoons salt                           |
| 2 1/8 | teaspoons minced garlic                  |
| 2 1/8 | teaspoons  black pepper — coarse ground  |
| 2 1/8 | teaspoons Italian seasoning              |
| 2 1/8 | teaspoons parsley flakes                 |
| 1     | ounce salt pork — diced                  |
| 2     | tablespoons olive oil                    |
| 4     | cans water — equal parts                 |

Heat oven to 350º.   Finely dice onions and salt pork. Put olive oil in Dutch oven. Add onions & pork to oil. Let mixture cook til onions are tender.  Stir every 5-to-10 minutes (do not burn, this mixture burns very quickly) After onions are slightly browned, remove pan from stove.  Add can of paste, 3 cans of puree, & equal parts of water.  Stir around when adding.  Add spices.  Stir & mix well.  Cover and place in oven. Cook for 4 hours. Remove from oven, remove cover and let cool. Refrigerate.  Freezing is not necessary as this sauce has a shelf life of 2 weeks, however, if necessary it freezes beautifully.

- - - - - - - - - - - - - - - - -

NOTES : Being that Gracie was of Italian descent,

spaghetti was a main-stay in our household. Every Thursday was "spaghetti day". It was the only day of the week that everybody loved to eat. With mom, dad, 5 kids, & mom's sister Julie who lived with us plus the dog, Skipper, someone always had to complain at dinner every night. But on Thursdays, the house smelled wonderfully with the sauce cooking all day, we were all practically salivating by the time supper was ready. If we got the chance to eat the fresh sauce in a bowl with a piece of homemade bread before supper, we really felt lucky. We could have eaten the whole pot of sauce that way. Even my Croatian father loved spaghetti and meatballs. Actually, he became an Italian through osmosis.

# Surprise Cookies

Serving Size : 24

|     |                         |
|-----|-------------------------|
| 1   | cup Butter — softened   |
| 1   | cup powdered sugar      |
| 1   | cup oats, rolled (raw)  |
| 1/2 | teaspoon salt           |
| 2   | teaspoons  vanilla      |
| 2   | cups flour              |

Mix together all ingredients to form a stiff dough.  On lightly floured board, roll or pat dough into a 7" x 11" rectangle (approximately) to 1/8" thick. Cut into 2 1/2" x 1 1/2" pieces.  Put on lightly greased baking pan.  Bake at 350 º  for 15 minutes. Watch carefully as they will get very brown.  When done, they should be golden brown. Cool on cooling racks.  Frost with your favorite butter frosting.  For holidays, color the frosting with colors for the season.

- - - - - - - - - - - - - - - - -

NOTES : When I was a teen-ager, one night as I was eagerly running out of the house to meet with my friends, my mother said to me, "Here, have a fresh cookie.  I found a new recipe and want to see how you like them."  As a teen-ager, my friends were more important than a freshly baked cookie, so, just to please her, I grabbed the cookie, tossed it into my mouth and started running out the kitchen door.  As I stepped onto the porch I stopped dead in my tracks, turned around and asked mother, "What kind of cookies are these?" They were so fabulous, I actually had the cookie take precedence over my friends. Right then I knew why they were called "Surprise Cookies". They don't look all that wonderful, but try them and I'm sure you'll agree with Gracie that they are quite a surprise. Each year for the holidays, now my daughter Jackie makes this cookie for our cookie exchange. Four generations have fallen in love with this cookie, because her daughters also love them.

# Tomato Salad

Serving Size : 8

|     |                                    |
| --- | ---------------------------------- |
| 4   | tomatoes, red ripe — wedged        |
| 1   | large onion — wedged               |
| 1   | medium green pepper — wedged       |
| 1/4 | cup olive oil                      |
| 1   | teaspoon salt                      |
| 1   | teaspoon black pepper              |
| 1   | teaspoon oregano                   |

Put all vegetable wedges into salad bowl. Add oil then seasonings. Toss together to mix seasonings. If desired, add more seasonings to taste. Mix this just before serving.

- - - - - - - - - - - - - - - - -

Serving Ideas : Serve with Italian or French bread.

NOTES : When we were kids, mother made this more often than a lettuce salad. The best part was dipping her homemade bread into the oil that would settle on our plates. Now-a-days when you go into an Italian restaurant, you're served warm bread to dip with olive oil as an appetizer. It tastes much better with the spices added to the olive oil. We didn't know that we were so fancy when all eight of us were reaching to scoop the oil from the bottom of the bowl so as not to waste any of the delicious juice.

# Tomato Soup Cake

Serving Size : 8

| | |
|---|---|
| 1/2 | cup shortening |
| 1 | cup sugar |
| 1 | egg |
| 1 | can  tomato soup |
| 1 | teaspoon baking soda |
| 1 | teaspoon baking powder |
| 1 | teaspoon cinnamon |
| 1 | teaspoon nutmeg |
| 1 | teaspoon cloves |
| 1/2 | cup nuts — chopped |
| 1/2 | cup raisins |
| 2 | cups flour |

## Frosting

Use recipe No. 3, Butter Frosting

Cream shortening and sugar.  Add egg and tomato soup then beat together.  Add dry ingredients, mix well.  Add nuts & raisins. Pour into 8"x8" pan which has been greased and floured on the bottom only.  Bake at 350 º  for 30-35 minutes.  When cake springs back at the touch, it is done. You may also prick it with a toothpick; if the toothpick comes out clean, it's done.  Cool on cooling rack.  After cool, frost with heavy chocolate butter frosting.

- - - - - - - - - - - - - - - - -

NOTES : This cake is an oldie. It's hard to believe how good the taste of tomato soup with chocolate frosting is. Mother's sister Florence, who was nick-named Peenie, why, we never knew, had this in her refrigerator all the time. When the chocolate frosting was cold from the refrigerator, it was so good, it tasted like fudge. She always piled on the frosting about 1 inch thick. Auntie Peenie was like a second mom to us. She had one son named Gene, who also had the nick-name of TeeTee, why, we never knew. (As I mentioned earlier in the book, most Rangers had nick-names; their origins were never known.) Auntie Peenie's house was like our house; we could come and go as we please, open the refrigerator and eat what we liked, sit around and play games, just like at home. Not many kids are lucky enough to have a second home in which they can feel so comfortable. Since our cousin, TeeTee, was an only child, and he was more like a brother than a cousin.

Mother's sister, Florence, also, known as Peenie, is pictured below at a surprise birthday party that we gave her. Her hair is still in curlers, she is surrounded by balloons, and laughing as usual. Mother had made the wonderful doll cake for her. We loved her like a second mother. She had never driven a car so whenever mother's car moved, Auntie Peenie was usually in it. We girls always had to go to her house and help her clean. Cleaning was such a big job in the old days. The carpets had to be taken outside and beaten while hanging over the clothes line; mattresses had to be removed and the old springs had to be cleaned with a brush; clothes in the closets and drawers had to be changed seasonally; and the furniture had to be polished with a paste wax, those were the days before Pledge had been invented. We were at each other's houses helping with the chores, but we had so much fun, we laughed all the time. We would clean late into the night, drinking coca cola in order to stay awake. We have such wonderful memories of our Auntie Peenie, she made us laugh.

# Tomatoes Ala Oil

Serving Size : 8

| | |
|---|---|
| 4 | tomatoes — sliced |
| 1/4 | cup olive oil |
| 1 | teaspoon salt |
| 1 | teaspoon black pepper |
| 1 | teaspoon oregano |
| 1 | teaspoon garlic — minced |

Slice tomatoes and arrange on round tray in circular manner. Drizzle oil all over tomatoes then sprinkle seasonings over all.

- - - - - - - - - - - - - - - - -

NOTES : This is a wonderful accompaniment, especially with an Italian meal. These kinds of recipes are sort of vague for the amount of servings. When serving a larger amount of people, slice more tomatoes and add a little more of all the seasonings. When you live with a person who is a natural cook, it is difficult to pin them down according to portions for serving sizes. They just seem to know what to do. The most difficult task when writing a cookbook about a wonderful cook is to try to get them to put amounts, portions, and sizes on paper. Everything was in Mother's head. Cooking was so second nature with her and she could never understand why it wasn't that way with everyone.

# Turkey Dressing

Serving Size  : 12

|  |  |
|---|---|
| 12 | cups dry bread — cubed |
| 1 | large onion — diced |
| 9 | stalks celery — diced |
| 1 | pound butter |
| 3 | cups broth |
|  | insides from turkey |
| 2 | teaspoons salt |
| 1 1/2 | teaspoons black pepper |
| 1 | teaspoon oregano |

Option 1: boil your gizzards, etc. (from the little bag placed inside  your turkey) for about 45 minutes; set aside to cool.  Saute' onion & celery in butter, stirring frequently, until transparent. Cool this mixture.  After broth and mixture are cooled, add to bread cubes.  Add seasonings then mix gently.  Stuff your bird with dressing; put the excess in a buttered baking dish and bake for 45 minutes.  When your bird is stuffed, allow a little more time for baking than suggested, perhaps 45 minutes to 1 hour more.

Option 2:  If you don't have the insides of the turkey (or chicken), or simply don't want to bother with boiling, you may use chicken bouillion or chicken base to make your broth.  When you're in a hurry it can expedite matters and minimize some of the mess that goes along with making dressing.

If you cut up your own bread cubes, it takes about a loaf of bread to make 12 cups; you may go the easier way and buy your bread already cubed.

The reason everything should be cooled is that by pouring hot broth and mixture over bread, it will make it very
soggy, and you want your dressing to be light and fluffy.

- - - - - - - - - - - - - - - - -

NOTES : Everybody has their own way of making dressing.  I think the secret to mother's dressing is the
oregano instead of sage.  Most people think that sage is
a must in dressing, but in actuality, it is very bitter.
Oregano is also a very strong spice, so be careful not to
overuse it.

# Walnut Potica

Serving Size : 45

|     |                             |
|-----|-----------------------------|
| 1   | pint half and half          |
| 3   | cups sugar                  |
| 1/3 | pound butter — melted       |
| 2   | pounds walnuts — ground     |
| 2   | eggs — beaten               |
| 1/4 | cup milk                    |

    * Filling is listed above
    * Dough is listed below

|     |                             |
|-----|-----------------------------|
| 2   | cups milk — scaled          |
| 1/2 | cup sugar                   |
| 2   | teaspoons salt              |
| 1/3 | pound butter or margarine   |
| 2   | packets yeast               |
| 1/2 | cup warm water              |
| 2   | eggs — beaten               |
| 6   | cups flour — * see note     |
| 1   | egg — beaten                |

Prepare the filling first as it is very hot and takes a while to cool. Bring half 'n half and sugar to a boil stirring occasionally. Remove from burner and add the butter and walnuts. Mix well. While the filling is cooling, prepare the dough. Put together in mixer bowl, the scalded milk, sugar, salt & butter. Cool to lukewarm. Put yeast into warm water and let sit. After mixture has cooled and the yeast has risen, add 2 beaten eggs and flour. *Note. If dough is too soft, more flour may be added in order to form a nice firm but soft dough. Put dough onto lightly floured table and knead into a nice round ball. the ball upside down, with creased side on bottom, so as to grease ball evenly. Cover with a cloth and set in warm area until dough rises double in bulk. (Do not over rise this dough as it will be difficult to work with.) Now for the fun part.........pulling or stretching the potica dough. Lay a clean tablecloth or sheet on a rectangular table. Sprinkle flour over entire cloth. Place dough in center of table and start pulling from the underside, pulling gently so as not to tear holes in the dough. Stretch dough over the entire table & let a couple of inches hang down on all sides to help anchor the dough. Be sure to start by anchoring down one corner of the dough so it will start hugging the table. After the dough is stretched, add 2 beaten eggs and the 1/4 cup milk to thin out your filling (this makes it more spreadable). With a rubbber scraper, spread the filling all over the dough completely filling the table from corner to corner.Prepare a pan so that after you finish rolling the potica, your pan is ready immediately so the dough doesn't sit and get dry. Completely grease a 9 x 13 pan. Lay waxed paper inside, the sides can extend off the edges and then grease down the waxed paper. Now your pan is ready to receive the potica. Trim off all excess dough hanging down from the edge of the table. Save it in a bowl. On one lengthwise plain edge, start to roll the dough over onto the top of table, keeping a small tight roll. Then lift the cloth under this start area and the potica will start rolling itself. As you lift the cloth, keep pulling it towards you so the potica doesn't fall on the floor at the end. Take your prepared pan and set it next to your strip of potica. Measure the length and then cut your first strip. You should have four strips of potica to place into this pan. To eliminate air bubbles in the dough, prick all the rolls with a fork, right to the bottom of pan. Spread last beaten egg over top of potica. Bake at 350 º for 1/2 hour, reduce heat to 300º for another

1/2 hour, then reduce to 250 º for last 1/2 hour.  Be sure
that potica is a dark golden brown.  Remove onto cooling rack and keep in pan until completely cooled.  To
remove, lay a long cooling rack on top and flip it out of
pan, then take another cooling rack and lay the potica
bottom onto a rack.  Cool completely before storing.
Wrap potica in plastic wrap and then foilplain.  It will
stay fresh in your refrigerator for 1 month.  It freezes
beautifully.  Freeze in small pieces so you may just eat
some when you want.

- - - - - - - - - - - - - - - - - -

NOTES : This sounds like a lot of work, but it really is
fun.  The stretching of potica dough is an art.  Once you
learn the trick, you will want to make it often.  I'm hoping
this art will not die.  I learned how to make this from my
mother who learned to make it from her mother-in-law
who was an immigrant from Croatia.  My father grew up
on this kind of food, so naturally my mother had to learn
how to make it. 50 years ago, when women were skilled
homemakers and cooking was a challenge to them, they
were eager to learn the crafts of cooking.  Now, in this
microwave world that we live in, a recipe this complicated might not interest some people.  But if you have
any love of the ethnic foods and hate to see all of our
old traditions die, you won't be sorry you tried this.
When mother had her restaurant, she should have
started a mail order potica business, but she was too
busy just cooking.

# STEPS IN MAKING WALNUT POTICA

The following pictures are the steps to making walnut potica. If your first potica is not successful, don't give up, keep trying.

STEP 1: The ball of dough is ready to rise.

STEP 2: Stretching the dough over the table by pulling from underneath.

STEP 3: Putting the filling onto the stretched out dough.

STEP 4: Spreading the filling over the dough.

STEP 5: Lifting the tablecloth and starting to roll the dough.

STEP 6: The finished potica roll.

STEP 7: Cutting the roll into strips and laying them in the prepared pan.

STEP 8: Gracie with her finished potica ready for baking.

STEP 2:

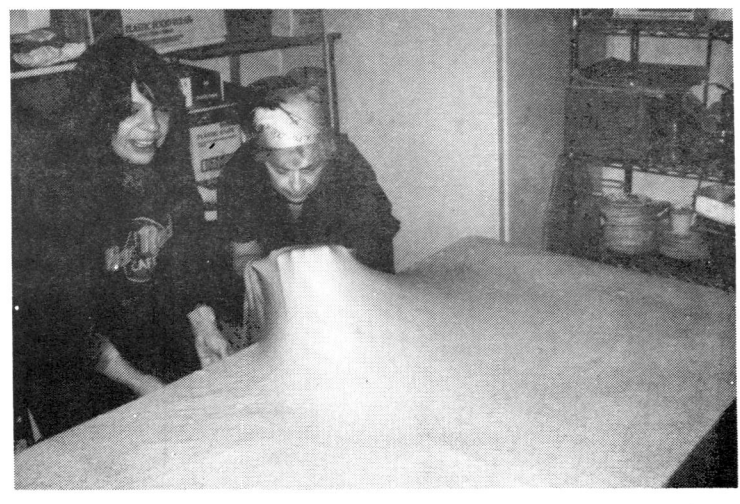

STEP 3:

STEP 4:

STEP 5:

STEP 6:

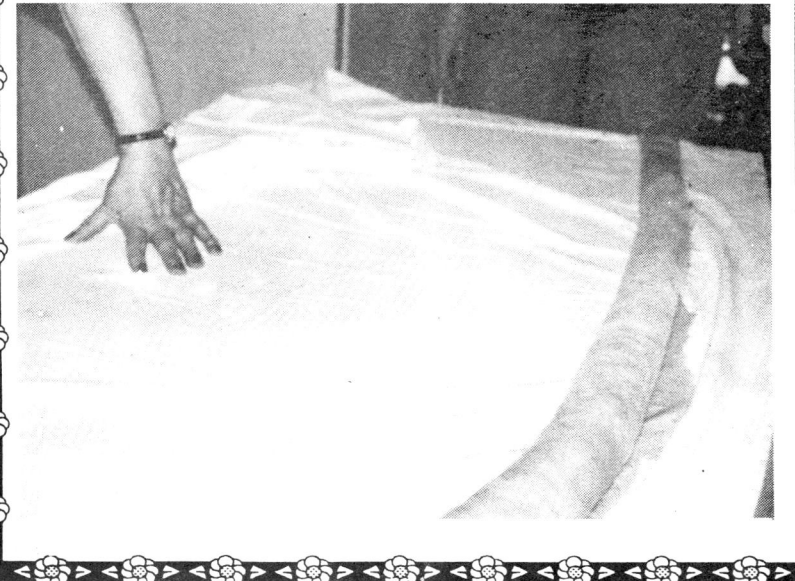

STEP 7:

STEP:8

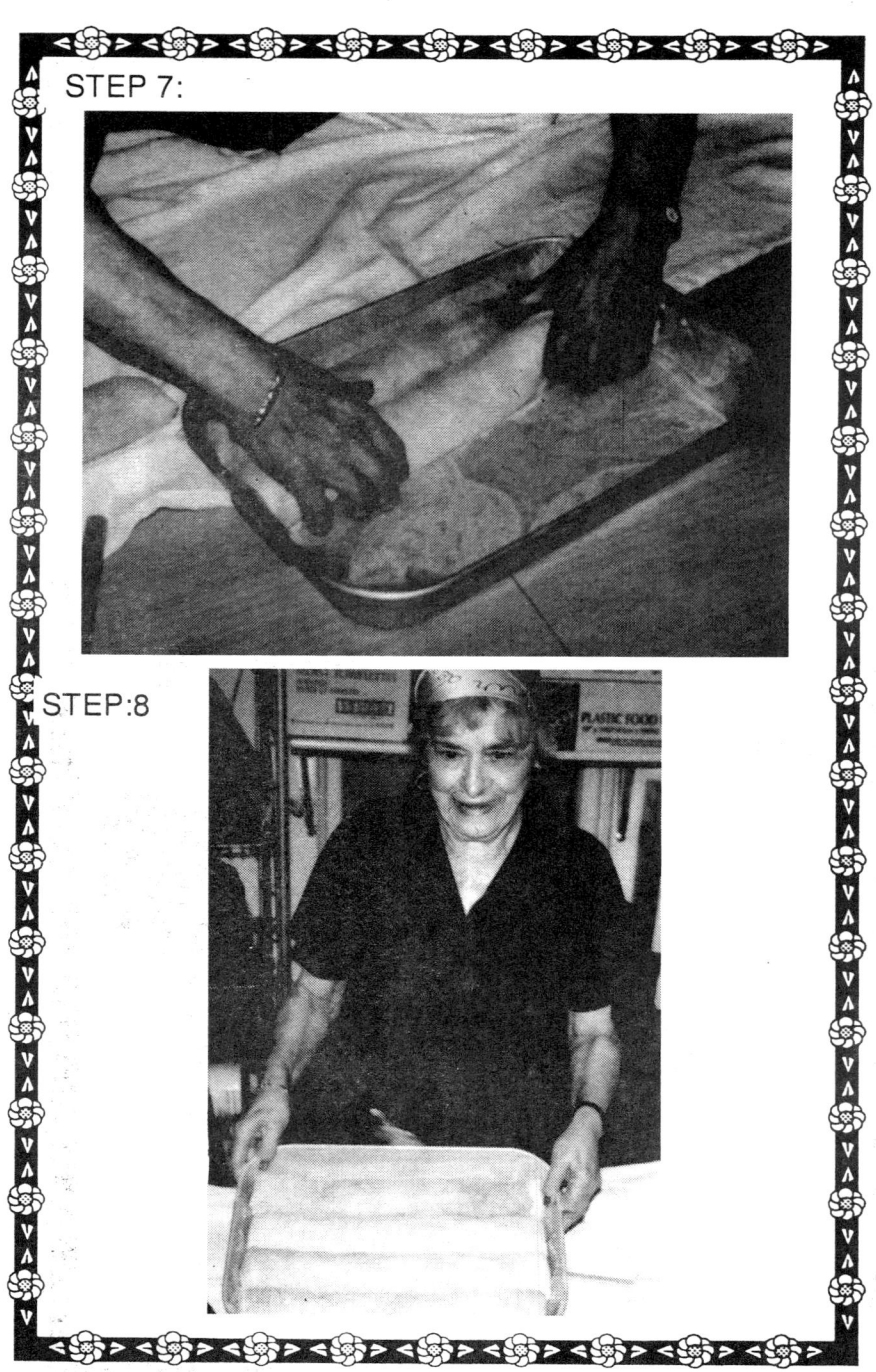

116

Pictured below is Gracie with her three daughters. Barbara Groves to her right, Sharon DeLeo standing behind her, and Joan Cornell to her left. All three girls adored their mother and are hoping to keep her love and art of "potica baking" alive by passing down the recipe to their daughters. The day we made the poticas for this book was a very special day. Two years previously, Gracie had been diagnosed with terminal lymphoma. She was determined to have her daughters and relatives learn to make her wonderful poticas. We called together relatives from California, Minneapolis, Duluth, the Range, and we had a "potica bake". Right from the very start of each recipe, she showed everyone how to make stretch, fill, and roll the doughs. As you read the recipes, you will find that the walnut potica dough is completely different from the apple and cheese. She was so proud to share her art with everyone. Grandchildren and great grandchildren, also, shared in the fun that day.

At the end of a long, weary day, Gracie is pictured with all of the tired potica bakers. For all the effort, let's hope they learned the skill of stretching a potica.

Back row: Jay & Dawn Sparks, (Gracie's grandaughter & husband); Jackie Phifer, (Gracie's grand daughter); Sharon DeLeo, (Gracie's daughter); Albert & Pat Gingerelli, (Gracie's brother & wife Pat who flew in from California for this day); David DeLeo, (Gracie's son-in-law).

Second row: Shelly Ceryance, (Gracie's daughter-in-law); Sarah Lundgren, (Gracie's granddaugh ter); Barbara Groves, (Gracie's daughter); Joan Cornell (Gracie's daughter.)

Front Row: Carolyn Gingerelli (Gracie's niece who drove  from Minneapolis for the event); Gracie; Irene Gingerelli (Gracie's sister-in-law, who also drove from Minneapolis).

This photo was taken by Sharon's dear childhood friend who drove from Duluth for this event, Elourine Maurine Alspach..

# White Bread

Serving Size : 2

|       |                           |
|-------|---------------------------|
| 2     | cups milk — scalded       |
| 1 1/2 | teaspoons salt            |
| 2     | tablespoons sugar         |
| 2     | tablespoons vegetable oil |
| 2     | packets dry yeast         |
| 1/2   | cup water — lukewarm       |
| 8     | cups flour                |

Scald milk, add salt, sugar, & oil in bowl, then cool. Add yeast to lukewarm water, set aside. When milk mixture is cooled, and yeast has risen, add flour and beat well, forming a nice firm dough. Turn out onto a floured board and knead for a few minutes; if dough is sticky, add a little more flour. Put into a greased bowl, oil the top of the dough, cover with a cloth and let rise til double in bulk. Cut the dough into two pieces, shape each piece into a loaf shape, put into greased bread pans, pierce with a fork to release the air bubbles, then let rise again til double in bulk. Bake in 375 º oven for 45 minutes or until golden brown. You can tell bread is done by turning over the loaf and knocking on the bottom; if it sounds "hollow", it's done. Cool on cooling racks. Store in plastic bags for freshness. It freezes very well. In fact, if you slice your loaf of bread before you freeze it, then you can just take out a slice whenever needed.

- - - - - - - - - - - - - - - - -

NOTES : Everybody loves homemade bread. When we were children, all we had was homemade bread. My best friend's family, the Marcaccini's owned the local bakery in Eveleth, and I loved going there so I could eat the bakery bread once in a while because we took our homemade bread for granted, and sometimes we wanted something else.  As I mentioned in my introduction, mother started baking bread when she was 14 years old; one would think that with all of the newer store bought breads, she would have been tired of it, but it was just a part of life that had to go on as usual. Old habits were always hard to break. Mother had the feeling that if she had done something once, and it was successful, she had to continue doing it whether or not it was a lot of work.

# White Fluffy Frosting

Serving Size : 1

|     |                  |
| --- | ---------------- |
| 1   | cup sugar        |
| 1/2 | cup water        |
| 2   | egg whites       |
| 1   | teaspoon vanilla |

Cook together the sugar and water, stirring until the sugar dissolves. Then cook without stirring until the syrup reaches 254 degrees on a candy thermometer, or when putting a spoon into the syrup, as you pull it out, a long string will "fly" on the tip of the spoon. While the syrup is cooking, beat egg whites until stiff. Slowly add cooked syrup to the egg whites; beating constantly until thick enough to spread. Add vanilla.

- - - - - - - - - - - - - - - - -

NOTES : This is a fabulous frosting; it never gets sugary after a few days like some boiled frostings do. Mother told me that she never really saw a recipe for this, that her sister, Mary, had shown her how to make this. When I was a young housewife, I had wanted to follow in my mother's footsteps and make the Devil's Food Cake with the White Fluffy Frosting for my daughter, Jackie's birthday, not anything fancy, just a cake. However, I struggled and ruined probably three batches of frosting and when my family arrived for the birthday party, there was my poor cake sitting without any frosting. My mother just laughed and within about 15 minutes the birthday cake was frosted and I received step by step instructions. Perhaps it was a little intimidating having such a good cook for a mother, but she was always wonderful about helping out.

121

# Wild Rice Prep

Serving Size : 12

1 pound wild rice
2 quarts water

Heat water to boiling. Add rice to boiling water. Cover and remove from heat. Let sit on cooling rack for 45 minutes to 1 hour. Drain cooled rice,set aside. You'll notice that it is already starting to open. Repeat this 2 more times. Since it takes a while for this process, plan on doing this early the day you need it, or the day before. Wild rice freezes very well. You may open your rice at any time, freeze it in a zip-lock baggie, then the day you need it, it will be ready to use. If you need it for a casserole, thaw it before mixing into your recipe, but you may put it into your soup frozen as it will thaw as soon as it touches the hot broth.

- - - - - - - - - - - - - - - - -

NOTES : Your friends will be so impressed with your wild rice. Mother learned this process from an old Finnish lady. Once you open your rice in this method, you will become very critical of all wild rice dishes served in most restaurants. It seems as though nobody knows how to open rice so completely, that not one kernel will be hard and crunchy. This is a fool-proof method for the lightest, softest wild rice anyone could ever taste. Because wild rice is very bland tasting, add lots of salt and pepper to any recipe when using it, except for hot dishes that have cream soups as a base. Canned cream soups are very salty, do not add much salt to your recipes.

# Notes

# ORDER FORM

## Carousel Sales, Inc.
812 7th Avenue
Two Harbors MN 55616

Ph: 218-834-3714

Visa/Mastercard accepted.

Please send me _____ copies of :

## "Iron Range Cooking with an Italian Mother"
by S. DeLeo

My payment of $10.95 per copy is enclosed. (Please add $1.50 to cover postage and handling.)

For Credit Card sales:

☐ Visa    ☐ Mastercard

Card No. _____

Exp. Date_____

Signature_____

Name_____

Address_____

City_____St____Zip_____